IN THE DRAGON'S TEETH

In the Dragon's Teeth

What the World Doesn't Know About China

June Mudan

iUniverse, Inc.
New York Lincoln Shanghai

In The Dragon's Teeth
What the World Doesn't Know About China

iUniverse books may be ordered through booksellers or by contacting:

iUniverse
2021 Pine Lake Road, Suite 100
Lincoln, NE 68512
www.iuniverse.com
1-800-Authors (1-800-288-4677)

Because of the dynamic nature of the Internet, any Web addresses or links contained in this book may have changed since publication and may no longer be valid.

ISBN: 978-0-595-45516-4 (pbk)
ISBN: 978-0-595-71008-9 (cloth)
ISBN: 978-0-595-89825-1 (ebk)

Printed in the United States of America

The views expressed in this work are solely those of the author and do not necessarily reflect the views of the publisher, and the publisher hereby disclaims any responsibility for them.

Some names, including my own, and locations have been changed to protect innocent Chinese people from government persecution.

Otherwise, the events recorded here are true and accurate.

This book is dedicated to my Chinese friend and fellow teacher, Robert whose actual Chinese name I cannot use for fear of what may happen to his surviving family members.
It is also dedicated to the millions of unknown
Chinese people who lost their lives
in the 1950s, 1960s and 1970s
during the Communist take over of China
led by Mao Zedong and others.
It is a major enumeration of crimes against humanity that to this day, little is known about, but Laogai (the Chinese equivalent of a death camp system) certainly needs to takes its place in the annals of atrocities against mankind on the level of
the Jewish Holocaust and Russian Gulag Archipelago.

With a heavy heart for China's past
and hope for humanity's future,
June Mudan

CONTENTS

Foreword..xiii

INTRODUCTION

Chapter One: How This All Came About........................... 3

Living in China *3*

Teaching the University Teachers *4*

His Promise Becomes My Promise..*6*

Why I Call Him Robert *7*

Chapter Two: The Difficult Writing Process................... 8

Returning to The U.S. *8*

A Slow Beginning..*10*

My New Goal======in The Same Sentence—The Holocaust, The Russian Gulag and Chinese Laogai *11*

Inner Conflicts and Fear for My Students...............................*12*

Chapter Three: I Find Another Survivor 14

At The Library...*14*

Harry Wu Speaks from His Own Experience...........................*15*

How Much Have People Cared?..*16*

Chapter Four: Looking At the Dragon 17

The Situation with China is so Different *17*

Politics is Alive and Well in The Economic World....................*17*

The Sleeping Dragon is Awake!!!!!!!!!! *20*

Chapter Five: Dangerous Details about the Dragon 22

Information I Learned While Living in China:..22
   Government Control of The Media...22
   Government Control of Education..24
   Government Control of Jobs...24
   Government Control of Housing..25
   Government Control of Marriage...26
   The Ultimate "Neighborhood Watch"..26
   A Whole Different World...27
   I Experienced Control Through The Velvet Gloved Hands of My Students..........28
   Living in Fear...29

PART ONE: JUNE GOES TO CHINA TO TEACH

Chapter One: Leaving Colorado Springs 33
Chapter Two: Minneapolis to Tokyo.....................................37
   June's Brief History of China—Part I......................................37
Chapter Three: Arriving in China...40
Chapter Four: The Drive from Shanghai 43
Chapter Five: My First Week in China 46
Chapter Six: Learning about Life in China—The Most Difficult
   "Camping Trip" of my Life...48
Chapter Seven: Learning about Life in China—Shopping 59
Chapter Eight: I Begin Teaching 63
   June's Brief History of China—Part II 66
Chapter Nine: My Great Teaching Idea 69

PART TWO: ROBERT'S EARLY LIFE IN CHINA

Chapter One: An Exceptional Beginning 75
Chapter Two: The Japanese Kill Many Chinese.........................79
   June's Brief History of China—Part III.....................................80

Chapter Three: From the Japanese to the Kuomintang 84

June's Brief History of China—Part IV 86

Chapter Four: A Successful Graduation from University 88

Chapter Five: The Hope of Communism Dies 91

June's Brief History of China—Part V 91

Chapter Six: A Hundred Flowers and Love Get Trampled 97

June's Brief History of China—Part VI 97

Chapter Seven: Life Deteriorates Even More 101

June's Brief History of China—Part VII 102

PART THREE: ROBERT'S LIFE IN CHINESE LAOGAI

Chapter One: The Jinquan Iron and Steel Company in NW China (1960) 107

Chapter Two: Moved to Xian (1961) 112

Chapter Three: An Unbelievable Trip to Shanghai in 1961 114

Chapter Four: My Romance Slowly Ends from 1962 to 1965 117

Chapter Five: The Famine Passes by 1965 120

Chapter Six: The Great Cultural Revolution in 1966 122

Chapter Seven: The Most Intense Time of the Cultural Revolution in 1970 125

Chapter Eight: Sent to Prison in 1970 128

Chapter Nine: Becoming Very Sick 132

Chapter Ten: An Example of Real Hunger 135

Chapter Eleven: Severe Crowding 137

Chapter Twelve: A Senseless Waste of my Life at Forty 141

Chapter Thirteen: Creativity Prevails 144

Chapter Fourteen:Unbearable Heat 147

Chapter Fifteen: A Trial—Again...149

Chapter Sixteen: A Different Prison in 1970 151

Chapter Seventeen: Work is an Improvement in 1971..................153

Chapter Eighteen: Officially Sentenced in 1972 156

Chapter Nineteen: Time on a Work-Farm in 1972 160

Chapter Twenty: Sick Body, Cured Spirit 163

Chapter Twenty-One: Back to the Work Unit in 1973 167

Chapter Twenty-Two: A Review of Robert's Family....................171

Chapter Twenty-Three: Harassment Continues...........................176

Chapter Twenty-Four: Great Upheavals in China in 1976 178

Chapter Twenty-Five: I Will Never Learn 181

Chapter Twenty-Six: Communist Politics Changes 184

Chapter Twenty-Seven: My Sister's Problems in 1980.................189

Chapter Twenty-Eight: My Lost Love 191

Chapter Twenty-Nine: True Love and a Full Life........................195

Chapter Thirty: Looking Back...197

Epilogue 201

In Appreciation...203

Bibliography 205

About the Author 207

Foreword

To date, many books have been written on contemporary China. Most of them were composed by scholars who aimed to shrewdly analyze China's political or economic landscape for their readers. We cannot, of course, say that these books are not valuable, for they certainly offer profound insight into some particular aspects of the Chinese phenomenon. June's book, however, is quite different. In writing it, she is in a very special situation: she is not a scholar or expert on China, and before traveling there she possessed only the knowledge and understanding of China that most typical Americans do. As such, she does not bring to this work the detached, impersonal assessment typical of academia. Rather, she offers the genuine and heartfelt revelations of a common American who had an uncommon encounter in China and who, from this experience, has grown to care about the country and its people very much.

June's perspective on China evolved from the time she spent there teaching English, and in particular, from one Chinese man, a fellow teacher, she met during that period. What this man shared with June, through his story, shocked her greatly—so much so that she decided to record what she learned and publish this book. In the pages that follow, June relates the disturbing revelations of this man to her readers. They include his experiences in the Laogai, China's version of the Soviet Gulag, a topic about which I personally know a great deal. I became quite familiar with life in the prison camps of the Laogai during the nineteen years I spent within them as a prisoner, subjected daily to forced-labor and "reeducation". The Laogai is incompatible with democracy. It is a tool needed by the Chinese regime to keep people like myself quiet, and it is emblematic of the human rights abuses prevalent in China today. Sadly, what June discovered from the man she met is that such experiences as this are not unique to him. He is but a common Chinese man, and unfortunately, many, many Chinese men his age have found themselves in similar situations.

China is undoubtedly becoming a "superpower", and its economy is steadfastly transforming into an open market-based system. Its repressive political character, however, has been maintained. The current situation is likely to lead the Chinese people in a new direction, although it is unclear what exactly it will be. To be sure, June, like us all, has her own political and moral views, shaped by her own experiences in life. Yet, this book does not attempt to promote any particular set of religious or moral values. Instead, June strives to honestly convey through her writing what she heard and saw in her eye-opening experience in China. The thoughts she has set down herein will answer fundamental questions for her readers in ways that her scholarly counterparts cannot. What is China? The answers June found to this question shocked her, and they are likely to shock her readers as well.

Harry Wu

INTRODUCTION

Chapter One:

How This All Came About

Living in China

I lived almost the entire year 2000 and into 2001 in East Central China, in a city of over one million people near the Changjiang River or Yangzi, as it is called in the West. It is located in a fertile and rich area, several hours by train, west of Shanghai. I taught English at a small little known university. I had over thirty offers to teach in China, some in Beijing, Shanghai and other huge cities, but I wanted to get to know Chinese people who were less sophisticated than those at a famous major university in a large well-known city. So I selected a "smaller" city which was still quite large by U.S. standards with a small university where the majority of students were first-generation college students (mostly due to Mao's mistaken goal to keep his people uneducated).

I feel that next to being a mother, (and many of you will know exactly what I mean by that) it was the greatest, most exciting and most educational experience of my life. I could talk for hours and perhaps write hundreds of pages about the people I met, the sites I saw, the wonderful experiences I had and all that I learned. It was truly an "experience of a life-time."

I am thrilled that you are interested in reading about my adventure. But you need to know from the start that, besides this being a travel story and fascinating comparison of cultures, it became much more significant and, at the same time, much less pleasant than I would have liked my adventure in China to be. The reason is that while there, I found myself immersed in well-kept dark secrets of intolerance, aberrant control, horror and death.

While in China, I saw the "dragon" in its entire splendor. I traveled to modern and majestic Beijing, historic Xian, bustling Chongching and rapidly changing Shanghai with its forest of skyscrapers. I visited many other places in China including the technical wonders of the Three Gorges Dam. I was able to go to Tibet, which the Communists say belongs to China because around 700 years ago, a Tibetan princess married the Emperor. I loved mysterious Guilin and felt that those strange little mountains became my friends whom I've missed ever since I left. I saw "heavenly" Hangzhou and Suzhou with their beautiful lakes and gardens. I climbed mountains in Tiashan and Huanshan. I could write hundreds of pages telling about the amazing sights of China.

But more importantly, I was able to know some of the off-spring of the dragon, which I saw as being the delightful, diligent and grateful students, both college age and older adults. I also met someone who told me from personal experience how sharp and vicious the dragon's teeth have been and, I must add, most likely still are. I believe that it is very important for Americans and others in the West to hear what I as told.

Teaching the University Teachers

After arriving at my Chinese university and meeting various members of the staff and administration, I was asked to teach Spoken English to the university teachers two evenings each week, in addition to teaching the university students during the day. I was, at first, a little intimidated by that prospect, but my attitude has always been, what's the worst that could happen? I couldn't think of anything. I knew that it would be a lot of extra work, but I was excited because my hope was that with a peer-group, I could more easily be myself and not have to always be in the role of "teacher." I hoped that I eventually could learn a lot too because the university teachers might come to the point of trusting me and being willing to share with me some of their real thoughts and feelings. This seemed like the greatest opportunity to get to know some adult educated Chinese people on a deeper level. This was better than I had dreamed possible and I was so happy that I didn't even think to ask for additional pay for the extra hours of work. That started my reputation of being "kind and generous," which I think were the nice words for less complimentary adjectives used behind my back. The Chinese have a special way of being respectful and disrespectful in the same smile. I love that quality because I have been cultivating it in myself since college and I was now learning from the "pros" who have been doing it for centuries.

The class, in fact, turned out to be as good as I had hoped. We did have many interesting, exciting and even some passionate discussions about many topics. I was able to share my ideas with the teachers and they came to a point of sharing some deeper thoughts and ideas with me. It was a teacher's "dream-class" with lively discussions, a flow of ideas and students looking forward to being there even after a hard day's work.

There was always good attendance. There were university staff members and teachers who joined the class in the weeks after it had started because I quickly got the reputation on campus of providing classes that were both worthwhile and *very interesting*. I eventually found out that many of the teachers were Communist party members so, in addition, I had the intellectual challenge of walking the tightrope of being "politically correct" in Communist China and yet being able to tell them that life in the U.S. and the free world was quite different from how they were living. I tried to educate them as much as possible without being critical in any way of Chinese Communism. Many times I amazed myself at how well I presented and handled difficult topics.

The English Department gave me unbelievable freedom with my teaching, but they had said that I needed to give my university students written homework. At first, I did not know what I could give as an appropriate written assignment for Spoken English. I, at first, joked about their spending so many minutes each week talking in English to one of the many trees on campus. The students already did this when it was time for one of their major exams in English. There were so many benches and large rocks around campus under trees where students could be found from early morning to night orally practicing English. It was while walking on the tree lined sidewalk to my apartment that a brilliant idea came to me: that if spoken English were written down, it would be called a "letter." So, I asked my students to weekly write to me a "love letter." I said that I used the words "love letter" because I hoped it would be from their hearts and that they would write interesting things about themselves and their lives because I was really interested in getting to know them. It turned out to be the best assignment there could be for my getting to know the students and sharing on a deeper level. Most of the students responded beautifully with sincere sharing of their lives.

I also gave this assignment to the university teachers, but I knew that they were too busy with their work and families. I did not expect many letters from them and as it turned out, I only received letters when there were things they had to say to me that they did not want to share with the others in the class, which was quite understandable due to Chinese politics.

But, there was one retired teacher who faithfully gave me a letter after each class. As we got to know each other better, he shared more and more about his life. He eventually presented me with information that would have a powerful impact on me and my perceptions of China. It would trouble me, compel me and would consume much time and energy for the next years of my life. Most importantly, it would make me feel that I had to rise to a task that I never thought I was capable of. I would write a book sharing what this retired Chinese teacher had told me about his life in China.

His Promise Becomes My Promise

I feel that I had to write this book because I learned that my adult student and eventual friend, Robert, had survived, as a political prisoner, about twenty terrible years in various Chinese labor and re-education camps called Laogai. Part of the reason he survived is that he had made a promise to himself that if he lived he would somehow get information about his life and what had happened to him, to other people, especially people in the West. I don't know what fantasies he had about how this would happen, but I, in time, became the person he had dreamed of meeting for over forty years. It started to feel like a "kind of" destiny that I had even come to this town and university, met with enough approval that I was asked to teach the teachers and was the type of sincere and curious person that I am. After time, I became the person who would carry his story to America and the West. He believed so much in America and in freedom and democracy. He actually idealized America and Americans, unfortunately much more than I think we deserve. It would please me greatly to be proven wrong on that account.

After reading his letters and then hearing him tell me about what had happened to him and how he felt, I promised him that I would get the story of his life published in the US. At the time I thought I would write magazine articles. I did not start out thinking of writing a book. I really didn't know how to do that or how much work it would take, but I decided that if he could survive such horrors, then I certainly could do whatever it took for me to write about it and tell others. Mine was the easier task, by far and some days, after struggling with the writing and publishing process, I remind myself of that fact.

Why I Call Him Robert

I want to explain my use of the English name, Robert, for the Chinese teacher. Most Chinese students, when studying English, take an English name. It is a fun thing to do and it often reflects how they see themselves and what they aspire to in life. I had students with names like "Michael Jordan," many named "Jack" after students saw the movie "Titanic" and one of my favorite names, "Pillar" because he saw himself as strong, sturdy and reliable, which he truly was.

Chinese names can be confusing, sometimes last name first, but not always and sometimes one name used twice. Whenever I recorded grades in my grade book I had the class monitor double check to make sure the correct person was getting the correct grade. Chinese names are also difficult for English speaking people to learn to pronounce. After I had taught for a few months and grew to know my students and care about them, I realized one day that I didn't even use their real names, just their chosen English names. I felt badly and made up my mind to change this, but often when I learned their Chinese names, an accomplishment for which I was proud, they smiled, complemented me and then said that they still wanted me to use their English names. Sometimes I would ask why? A puzzling explanation centered on the fact that the use of a name is different in English. From what I understand if a person is talking to someone in Chinese, they are not addressed by name as we do in English. I finally asked one student, "What does your mother call you when she talks with you?" He said, "She usually doesn't call me anything or she may occasionally refer to me as son."

The students really seemed to like how we use a name and how I always addressed them many times by their English names as we were talking. Some said that it made them feel like I really cared, that they were more recognized as a person and that it often felt like an endearment. So, I will use the English name, Robert, because that is the name he chose and what I always called him in China.

CHAPTER TWO:

THE DIFFICULT WRITING PROCESS

Returning to The U.S.

After returning to the U.S. in 2001, I underwent quite the culture shock. It was much more troubling than the culture shock I felt going to China. My plane landed in San Francisco and I was soon helping my daughter and our three dogs (my Chow and her two huge Rottweilers) make a difficult move from California to Kansas City, Missouri. It took two days to drive by car from California to Colorado Springs where my dog and I were dropped off. That is where I had lived and my car was being stored. I spent some time with my son, grandson, and friends. I also checked on my house in the Colorado Rocky Mountains. Then after driving to Kansas City where I left my dog again with my daughter, I flew to Florida to see my parents.

Within about one month of returning from half way around the world, I had traveled from the West Coast to almost the East Coast. First, I had driven with my daughter and our three dogs across the western half of the country through some rough and breath-taking mountain terrain. We were pulling a camper filled with over 200 lbs. of my belongings that I had used while in China and some of my daughter's "necessary belongings" that she didn't want the movers to take, plus two big bags of different kinds of dog food, one kind for each type of dog and a great assortment of dog toys and treats. I felt like we were a typical American family with so much stuff that we needed to pull a trailer behind us to haul it all with us. And our "typical family" was over half "non-human" and just as spoiled as we were.

In Colorado while visiting family and friends, I crossed, using four-wheel drive, the highest paved mountain pass in the United States in the deep snow of winter. I later drove in one day on an unbelievably smooth interstate across Kansas and finally flew to the gulf coast of Florida where my parents live. I was over-whelmed with being back in America.

I was struck with our American mobility, having my family spread across the country and everyone wanting to see me a.s.a.p. I thought very little of crossing our vast country. It was not only comfortable, but it didn't seem to be expensive. In China, most of my trips to other cities were difficult "projects" that took careful planning, great preparation and were unbelievably exhausting. The railway system in the rest of the world may seem amazing and relatively convenient, but not compared to America's automobiles and super inter-state highways. We are so spoiled to be able to pack ourselves and much more than we need into our cars, leave, stop, eat, rest and spend the night, all as we please.

While in China I almost always took students with me when I traveled and it was surprising how expensive they thought the travel was. The student who took me to the Three Gorges Dam was going to stay on campus that summer because he could not afford the train and boat fare to go home. To me the cost seemed so small and was certainly well worth it for the opportunity to live with his Chinese family for one week. The student who flew to Tibet with me had the first plane flight of his life. It brought me so much joy to share this exciting experience since I flew for the first time when I was ten years old and my children flew for the first time as infants. Travel in this world is much more varied than we realize and in the US we take what we have for granted, not realizing how wonderful it is and how truly fortunate we are.

Americans expect so much from life and always with the immediacy of fast food. We own so much stuff that we hope will improve our lives, but instead it makes us stressed. Instead of making our lives more convenient and comfortable, the "stuff" too often makes life more complex and overwhelming. I had come to see that other people in this world have problems mostly due to poverty; very long hours of work to make a living and unsanitary conditions that are common in most of the world. These are not major problems for most people in the US. But, it appeared to me that most often in America we create problems and difficulties for ourselves because we do not have the wisdom to live simple satisfying lives. We have the mistaken idea that *more* is always better. I did not like what I saw being home in America and I questioned how I had been living and how I might live differently with these new insights.

My point in saying all of this is that I found it much harder to readjust to the complex life in America than it was for me to adjust to my simpler, but more difficult life in China. I often referred to my year in China as the most difficult "camping trip" of my life. There were many inconveniences and discomforts which I will tell you about later, but the wonderful things that happened far out-weighed the hardships and now I have, for the most part, the most precious memories that live in my mind and heart.

A Slow Beginning

For many reasons, months went by before I began writing. I had made a commitment in China to do something that I knew would push my skills to their limit and maybe beyond. I knew that I might have bitten off more than I could chew, but under those circumstances, what does a person do? It reminded me of the children's joke, how can a person eat an elephant?===one small bite at a time. My course of action became taking little bites. At first, I wasn't writing a book, but just some paragraphs or maybe a page or two. As long as I was making progress and moving in the right direction, it was OK.

I began the long writing process by looking over the letters that I had been given in China, notes that Robert gave me and information that I had put in my laptop to bring back to the US. I had worried that I might have problems leaving China with the information that I had, but absolutely NOTHING of mine was checked either leaving China or entering the US.

Robert's English, though it seemed reasonably good when speaking in class or with me, was very hard to read. His handwriting was hard to figure out and the cheap flimsy paper, so common in China, made it even more difficult. If I had known what a difference it would make, I would have bought high quality paper for Robert and insisted that he use it on one side only, but I didn't know that he would write so much for me or that things would happen as they did. None of this was planned, but as it unfolded it took on an energy and life of its own.

It also took me a long time to figure out that often he did not present his thoughts in a chronological order. He went back to a previous time when he suddenly remembered something he had left out. Often he gave the outcome of a situation as he told of the situation in whatever order it came to mind. There were some things that I simply did not understand what he was referring to, but I started plowing through the material.

By this time, I also had a full-time job, family and other obligations, but my biggest obstacle was my own fear of being able to accomplish writing a book. This is one of the greatest personal growing experiences of my life. So many times I said to myself—"just take one more small bite of the elephant" and "you HAVE to do this for Robert, he is depending on you." Then I would think of him being cold, hungry and sick, almost dying and I would forge ahead with an ever growing commitment to tell his story.

I feel that I need to explain, at this point, that I did graduate from a major university, even with honors. I have two Masters' degrees and I wrote a thesis for one of them. I have accomplished some written academic tasks in my life. But, being well-educated and writing a book, like this, is not necessarily the same thing, especially writing about such a serious topic. Writing this book will, without a doubt, top my list of difficult accomplishments in my life. Some days I honestly wish that I hadn't made such a commitment, so I could just relax and enjoy myself during my spare time, instead of spending endless hours at my computer. But, the truth is that I couldn't stop writing for long, and not only because I had made the promise to Robert, but also because the more I learned about the Chinese Laogai, the more important I came to believe it is for others in the West to know about it.

It happened by chance or "an act of fate" that I was given this very interesting information and regardless how inadequate I feel or how many times it takes me to rewrite each sentence, I must follow through and tell others.

My New Goal======in The Same Sentence—The Holocaust, The Russian Gulag and Chinese Laogai

Sometimes I would, deep inside me, feel another motivation for writing when I would hear the mention of the Jewish Holocaust or of the Russian Gulag. In America there are many programs on TV about the Holocaust. It was amazing how often things were said relating to those past horrors with the statement that if we don't learn from history, we may repeat it. When either the Holocaust or Russian Gulag would be brought up, there was often reference to the other atrocity. I would wait to hear next the mention of what had happened in China, but there was never such a word. "The Chinese Communist labor reform camps (Laogai-dui) have been in existence for over forty years, and in every respect—in terms of scope, cruelty, and the number of people imprisoned—they rival the Nazi and Soviet systems." (Wu, 1992, xii)

I think that it is amazing how the Chinese Laogai have remained such a secret. I can't believe that something so terrible can remain unspoken of in this day and age of open communication in most of the world. "Yet the experience of China's prison camps remained largely undocumented, a forbidden area, its secrecy maintained by strict regulations but also by the reluctance of survivors to reveal their most painful and humiliating memories. Harry Wu determined to break that silence." (Wu, 1994, Preface) When people read what he had to say, why weren't they offended and horrified about what happened in China? Why didn't the word spread like other secrets have? How has it remained so shrouded? It makes what I have to tell you that much more important, but also more difficult because I'm revealing a huge dark secret of a government, a political ideology and a culture that has already been ignored and I don't know that I can have a greater impact. I wish I had a Ph.D. in Chinese Studies or was some kind of political or historical authority who could somehow demand more attention.

I am simply an American teacher who went to China to teach English. My qualifications for writing are strong, but simple: I was there, I really wanted to learn about the people, I earned their trust and then listened to what was shared with me. Then, due to my own shock, horror, and amazement, I found myself develop a strong need to tell you what I was told. I did not plan any of this. I feel uncomfortable being in this position, but I must try to have as many caring humans as I can, hear what I was told.

I wish that the entire world already knew about the Chinese Laogai. I would then just be contributing additional information about another person who suffered at the hands of the Chinese Communist Government. It would make things much easier for me.

Inner Conflicts and Fear for My Students

I also want you to understand some of the conflicting feelings that I have had while writing. I loved my year in China and I grew to love the Chinese people. My personal experiences in China were great. The students were as kind, loving and hard working as any teacher could dream of having. My Chinese University and the staff of the English Department did their best to make me comfortable, safe and very welcome. People on the streets (and believe me there were many of them) were friendly and respectful. The families of many of my students welcomed me into their humble homes or small apartments and treated me with heart-warming hospitality. So many Chinese people treated me with respect, loving kindness, warm hospitality and great generosity. I loved the Chinese people because they were easy to love. So many people who I met are still dear to my heart and I do not want to cause them any grief, embarrassment or anything worse from their government. As memories of various students come into my mind, I worry that they may have to pay a terrible price for simply being my friend and my writing this book. This alone is an indication of the level of fear and retribution beyond our experience in the West.

I feel pain because I have *terrible* things to tell of what the Chinese Communist Government did to my friend, Robert and people he knew. And I fear that it may also happen to the people I know because of my telling what happened to him. There are estimates that similar or worse things may have happened to fifty million Chinese. Allow me to repeat that number so you know it is not an error. I said 50 million people. And many believe that it is continuing to happen to this day. (Wu, 1996, 55)

I have come to the conclusion, with the help of a friend that I must tell you the information Robert told to me without making political commentary. Yes, I can tell right from wrong and I can recognize horror, as well as you can. But the truth is that there is so much that I do not know about Chinese history, government or politics. Living somewhere and being an "expert" on that place are two very different things. After my year, I felt that I had just scratched the surface of the cultural differences. I don't want to give you the impression that I am a "China expert" or am speaking as some great authority on China. And yet, I do not want my feeling of lack of authority to keep me from writing what I believe the entire world needs to hear.

My goal is to tell you about Robert's life as he related it to me and that is what I am an expert on. He told me in all honesty and seriousness, often with tears and great humiliation. I do not doubt anything he said because many of the horrors he repeated to me verbally and with shame, to make sure that I understood exactly what he meant. I am reporting it with accuracy and great care. I have spent years going over my words to make sure they are correct and accurate. My commentary and conclusions will be limited because it really doesn't matter what I think or feel compared to the facts and information that I present. I hope that you will think carefully about what I say and provide your own commentary and conclusions as you are reading. My ultimate dream is that someday there will be actions that concerned people take.

CHAPTER THREE:

I FIND ANOTHER SURVIVOR

At The Library

After a few weeks of working with the material that I had, I went to the public library to find if there were any books about Chinese concentration camps or a Chinese Gulag like Alexander Solzhenitsyn had written about in Russia.(Solzhenitsyn, 1985) I found in the library one author who had written a book called *Troublemaker—One Man's Crusade Against China's Cruelty*, written in 1996. (Wu, 1996) The man's name is Harry Wu. I eventually decided that I had to buy a copy of my own to study and write in. Then I found that he had other books called, *Laogai—The Chinese Gulag*, written in 1992 (Wu, 1992), and *Bitterwinds—A Memoir of My Years in China's Gulag*, written in 1994 (Wu, 1994). I was able to order them to study, write in and refer to.

On many days, these books have become an additional inspiration that keeps me going. I was shocked by the magnitude of what Harry Wu had written. I had thought that my friend, Robert, was part of a small group of people that the Chinese Communist Government persecuted in their capricious and cruel ways. I did not know the extent of the horror. Now I felt even more compelled to do my part so the world knows about these men and what they experienced and about other people who were not as lucky and did not live to tell their stories. These people were so horribly treated not because they had done anything wrong or had committed crimes, but because they had fallen out of favor with the Communist leaders in their area. This government and these officials held such absolute power over another person's life, that they could allow the person to live a normal life, destroy a life by making it a living hell, or maybe even take a person's life completely and sometimes painfully. The choice was up to them. There doesn't seem to be any system of "checks and balances" in Communist China. How I would hate living under such a threat, such uncertainty and capriciousness and I worry about the students who are dear to me and I had to leave under those conditions.

In the US we so often speak of being "empowered," as women, as workers, as teachers, as students, whatever. In America we are into "personal rights," "personal power", the "individual," but in China, life is as different from this as it can be. Our experiences in this area are hardly within their comprehension. They don't know how different our lives are. You will also find that some things that I say are hard to believe or don't make sense. There are huge differences in this world and you are about to learn about some of the most terrible.

Harry Wu Speaks from His Own Experience

Harry Wu says in *Troublemaker* in 1996 that, "The Chinese government has admitted that ten million people have been sent to the camps since the Communists took over in 1949. In 1995, officials said there were 1.2 million workers in 685 camps. This is a ridiculously low figure. I estimate that more than fifty million people have been sent to the laogai since 1949. We currently have records of 1,155 camps, with between six million and eight million prisoners in them. I believe that perhaps 10 percent are political prisoners, people who said the wrong thing at the wrong time. The world knows only the tip of the iceberg.... Millions of people have been lost in laogai. Every one of those lives is precious. The Chinese people have a saying, "We're not looking for the tree but also the forest." The Chinese preoccupation with the majority has led to abuses by dictators like Mao Zedong. Individuals cannot stand up. The forest is too important. I speak for the trees. Each one has a name, a face, a soul, a family. Some of them were my friends. How can I neglect them now that I have freedom? This is my cry. This is my mission." (Wu, 1996, 14)

I also feel that I cannot forget what happened to Robert or keep it to myself.

Harry Wu goes on to say that when he returned to China in 1995 to learn about the current conditions of the labor camps, "I was over there representing the millions of Chinese people who have lived and died in the labor camps. I went back for all my friends who died while I lived. I went back to see the labor camps where I was a prisoner for nearly two decades.... I am trying to be a witness for millions of others just like me."

(Wu, 1996, 12)

How Much Have People Cared?

Harry Wu has had the opportunity to appear on American television, including NBC's 60 Minutes. He has been asked to speak before the California Legislature and the United States Congress. He has also taken his message to many European countries. (Wu, 1996, 291, 296–297)

He has tried his best and continues to work with all his time and energy. Perhaps he was the first person with tales of horror and because of the organization he founded, Laogai Research Foundation in Washington D.C., more stories are being told by other Chinese people.

Now I, as an American and certainly an outsider to Chinese politics and perhaps a more objective person, have to add what I have learned because I believe with all my heart that what happened in Chinese Laogai needs to be known as much as we know about other atrocities against mankind. It is often said that if we as humans do not learn from history, we will be doomed to repeat it. China has no right to keep its personal monstrous holocaust a secret, especially with the position that China is now gaining in the world. The world needs to know in all openness and honestly what the Chinese Communist Government was capable of doing in the past so we can have more accurate understanding of the present and make better educated decisions in the future.

I was definitely not on a mission to find out anything bad about China. I went to China to have an adventure and to help its people. I found out a terrible secret and I need to tell my country and others in the world what I was told. I want to share this because America and the world needs to know what is lurking in China's past and maybe also in the present. We, in America, have come to like the Chinese dragon and especially, all its low-priced wares, but we also need to know about its sharp vicious murderous teeth and how they have been used to maim and murder millions.

CHAPTER FOUR:

LOOKING AT THE DRAGON

The Situation with China is so Different

It doesn't take a political genius to see the huge differences between Nazi Germany, the Soviet Union and China. When details about the Holocaust became known we had just conquered Germany in the worst war the entire world had ever seen. It was great to find out what a truly horrible enemy we had subdued. We were not only the victors, but we were also saviors of millions of innocent people who were freed from Nazi concentration camps.

When Solzhenitsyn wrote his *Gulag Archipelago* (Solzhenitsyn, 1985), we already knew that we had a terrible enemy on our hands with the Soviet Union. He provided additional evidence that the Cold War was even more valid than we had thought. We were not only saving ourselves and the free world from the horrors of Communism, but perhaps we could be saviors of millions of innocent people being held in Soviet labor camps.

China is in an entirely different position in the world.

Politics is Alive and Well in The Economic World

China is no longer our Communist enemy like when Mao ZeDong made threats of nuclear war. I can still remember hearing as a little girl about the starving children in China, so I needed to clean off my dinner plate. But I also fearfully remember hearing my grandmother vividly tell that China could drop an atomic bomb on us and then had such a great population that their millions of soldiers could takeover what was left of America. I feared China, as a small child and then grew to later fear the Soviet Union as we, for years, practiced atomic bomb drills at school, at least as often as fire drills. I can still tell you the different places our classes were assigned to go in the basement of my elementary school incase of a nuclear blast.

Mao is long dead, though his body is still being viewed by thousands daily in a building on Tiananmen Square. (I would not go to see it for many many reasons.) Few Americans today remember his frightening statements about the aftermath of nuclear war. Mao said that although half of the human race might be annihilated in a nuclear war, so would western imperialism. He believed that millions of Chinese people would survive and could create a civilization a thousand times better than the capitalist system. That is part of the reason he encouraged such an increase in the population of China that has now resulted in the "one child policy" to get the population more under control. Many times when people would ask me what is the biggest difference between the U.S. and China. I would reply, "one billion people." I could not believe how a normal day of shopping in the downtown reminded me of the Fourth of July in America when the fireworks was over.

Today China, with all those workers, has become a major economic power in the world. The balance of trade is monthly, millions of dollars in its favor. Probably it is accurate to say that the U.S. is China's best customer and they are "our provider of choice." It seems that almost everything that we buy today is "Made in China." Today, at least 70 percent of non-food items sold in Wal-Mart stores have a Chinese component. Ted Fishman, author of the book China, Inc., notes "there's a Chinese component in virtually every aisle you walk in Wal-Mart and Wal-Mart is the conduit for all of the output of the Chinese economy directly into American Lives." Wal-Mart imports an estimated eighteen billion dollars in products from China each year. Experts believe Wal-Mart is China's eighth largest trading partner importing more goods each year than entire countries such as England and Russia. I do not believe that Wal-Mart can say with any certainty that nothing it sells was made in Chinese Laogai.

Many Chinese prisons are also companies. "China's rulers change the names of their prisons to make them sound like factories. The prison factories and prison farms have double addresses, double names, but Westerners still visit them and never ask about the abject men and women in the blue shirts hunched over the assembly lines. Many of them are not ordinary workers but prisoners who have been reduced virtually to slaves. The labor of Chinese prisoners is more valuable now than it has ever been." (Wu, 1996, 13) They may also have two entrances, one entrance and area is like a corporation and then a less obvious but large area is the prison. We may all think that this is OK because we also have prison inmates working in America. Of course, it's good for prisoners to work and not sit around all day. But, what is significant is what is considered a "crime" in China. People in Chinese prisons may be robbers and murders, but other people have done *NOTHING* illegal except disagree with the government or in the many cases that you will hear about, be in the wrong place, near the wrong person in power.

We have no obvious reason for wanting to think bad things about China. I don't expect that what I have to say will be popular, especially with American discount shoppers. There are actually more reasons to want to over-look Laogai in China. They are partly responsible for some of our cheap prices because prisoners do not have to be paid as other laborers are paid. They do not need quality food or living conditions. They are the cheapest labor possible.

Many people will rationalize that after all, this is the Chinese government dealing with their own people. If that's what they want to do with their own people, why should we get involved? People may think: "is it really any of our business what they did, or even do?" Others will rationalize and say that what happens "behind closed doors" or behind "Chinese walls" should stay that way. Is it really our concern? "Bad things happen all over the world." We know that the Chinese Communist Government isn't into human rights, but this is their own people they are hurting. If they were hurting someone else, it might be different and we might do something. "OK, well Tibetans look like Chinese!" The rationalization can go on and on and on.

Besides, really what can we do about it?? There is nothing we can do. We have no power, control or even influence in these matters. With the memory of that photo of Tiananmen Square still in our minds, thanks to that brave student who defied the tank, we know that no one in China besides those in absolute power has any power, except the very bravest who are willing to die. Life appears to be cheap and the individual of little value. We seem to be buying into that concept in relationship to China more than ever before. Maybe if we think about it, more than we should??

The Sleeping Dragon is Awake!!!!!!!!!!

People can rationalize all they want and they will, but I must do my part so that you will have information and a new sense of understanding of China. We know that China has often been portrayed as a "dragon," and it has been a "sleeping dragon," but it is now awake and on the move. It has done and may continue to do what dragons are known to do. They have fierce sharp teeth and they use them. Sometimes they just use them to threaten and frighten, but soon you will hear too of how the teeth have maimed and murdered innocent people.

In his own words, Harry Wu also said: "I want to tell you about the camps in China. For nineteen years, I was one of those prisoners, held for vague offenses against my homeland. My captors said they wanted to reform me, but really what they wanted was to work me until I dropped. I was lost in the camps that are strategically scattered all over China, where millions of prisoners produce goods for Chinese industry. For my purposes, I call the entire system Laogai.... Laogai— the phrase burns my soul, makes me crazy, makes me want to grab Americans and Europeans and Australians and Japanese by the shirt and scream, 'Don't you know what's going on over there?' I want the word Laogai to be known all over the world in the same way that gulag has become synonymous with the horrors of Stalin's prison system." (Wu, 1996, 13)

I think that Harry Wu may have, like Robert, idealized Americans, and also Europeans, Australians and the Japanese. It appears now that not many people seem to care. But, I will be an optimist too and believe that sometimes people can rise to their potential, if provided enough information and out-rage for the sake of humanity.

What is most remarkable and unbelievable is how something like this has remained almost unknown to the rest of the world. In America we know so much about our government because of the media. Nothing can remain a secret for long. But, there are two huge factors that make such secrets possible in China. We, in America, hardly have a clue about these things : CONTROL and FEAR. I will share with you some personal experiences that I have had with these concepts in China. Realize that they are so foreign to us. The examples that I give may seem minor and trivial, but think about them for awhile, put yourself into these issues and ask how you would feel about them, *if it were your life.*

It is also significant that Chinese Banks have loaned more money to America and American businesses than most knowledgeable politicians want to think about or admit. We are becoming more ingratiated, entangled and indebted to

China. I don't think that we really know what we have gotten ourselves into. We need to learn before it is too late for us.

Chapter Five:

Dangerous Details about the Dragon

Information I Learned While Living in China:

Government Control of The Media

The Communist government ultimately controls much of life in China. We, in America, not used to government control, have no idea what this means or how that is possible. We experience total freedom to come and go, study and work without anyone in the government knowing or caring what we are doing, unless laws are broken. Of course also, at tax time our government has its greatest interference when making sure it has its fair share of our income to run the country. In China there aren't "taxes" as we know it. The government essentially "withholds" everything and you are paid what they want you to have. It sure makes our tax system seem a lot better.

In China life is so different because almost everything is not only known, but controlled and there is an underlying fear because the Chinese people know what power the Communist government has and the fact that there are NO HUMAN RIGHTS given or guaranteed by their government, a constitution or Bill of

Rights. When thinking in terms of China, we can realize how truly precious these things are that we vaguely remember studying in a high school social studies class. Human rights can truly make life worth living and a lack of them can make it unbearable.

Although our media has its faults and limitations, it does have the freedom to tell us anything. The Chinese government totally controls the media in China. People are only told what the government allows them to be told. Often it was laughable to hear the international news in China given in English and the spin the government puts on life in the US and free world. I sometimes said, "like anybody is going to believe that!?!" But, most people in China do, because that's what they are told.

The Internet is having a great impact on life in China. People have a new way to gather information and it can't be totally controlled, although I often was told that many web-sites cannot be accessed in China. I enjoyed it immensely when my students would check on the Internet if what I had told them in class was true. For example, one day I had said that fourteen of the fifteen most polluted cities in the world were in China. My students hadn't heard that and didn't like it that I had made such a terrible accusation. They knew that Americans created the most pollution, but they had no idea of how bad pollution is in China. To them, we in the West were totally at fault for "destroying the planet" and, of course, China was innocent and blameless.

One of the strangest things I experienced in China is how different the sun looks in the sky. It is always filtered by so much pollution that you can see a ring at its edge. I cannot find the words to accurately describe the great difference there is. The Chinese people, of course, assume that this is the norm for all over the world, which it definitely is not. How would they know any differently?

I still remember the night that I asked in my university teachers' class how many people had been outside of China. Only one man volunteered that he had been out of the country, but I know others also had been, but weren't brave enough at this point to enter into the discussion. Then I asked him about the way the sun looks in China compared to Europe where he had been. I let him be the one to explain to the class the difference and how it is related to the severe pollution in China. We had quite the discussion that night, but too often my teacher-students spoke in Chinese to each other because it was beyond belief what they were hearing. They had to ask for clarity and share their disbelief in their native language. I also think that they were so troubled that they didn't want me to know how little they were aware of the truth and didn't want to believe it.

My students often told me to be careful when sending e-mail. I did not believe that millions of messages could be monitored. Since my return to the US, I have learned that they and their fear were appropriate and correct. I did not believe what Chinese Communist control was like even when I was living under it.

Government Control of Education

I really became aware of how the government controls the educational system. A student gets into a university by scoring high on tests and then, based on the tests, they are told what their major will be. I had many students tell me that they are in fields of study that they don't like, but there is no choice, but to work hard and do well, because there is only one chance for higher education in China. You cannot drop out or flunk out and get another chance. I had a student tell me how he had been planning his suicide because he could not go home from school as a failure. One of the students I got to know and love, one of the kindest, most gentile and loving young woman, missed being able to go to medical school because she had been up all night before the test, taking care of her sick mother. There is no such thing as a "re-take" on a different day. She is now not in a people-oriented field like she wanted, but is working with computers, which seem boring and unfulfilling to her. I could sense when she spoke with me how her young spirit was broken. Both China and she have lost out in this process. The stories I heard were too common and numerous for me to tell them all.

Government Control of Jobs

The government also controls most jobs. You don't work or make a living without the approval for the job by the Communist Government. There are some open jobs that people can interview for, but even these have great restrictions. If you get into the "free market" you forgo a position with the Communist Party. Many students asked my advice about their becoming a Communist and their fear of not becoming one. They wanted to know if freedom and the free market really work. They thought that as a teacher in America, I not only worked for the government, but was told where and what I would be teaching. They could not believe that I have lived in six different states and was able to go to a different state if I wanted to and then get a job there. Students had come from many locations in China to attend our university, but when school was over they had to return to their home or at least their home province. A person cannot live wherever they want in China.

They really don't understand how a free market works in the United States, a totally free country. Our system is unbelievable to the Chinese and their system seems beyond comprehension to us. They actually think that government control is the only way life can exist. Most of the time, we assume that the whole world lives with the freedoms that we enjoy and take for granted. Likewise, the Chinese assume that our lives are not so different from their lives except that we have more money. I tried to be respectful when talking about such differences to be as factual as possible and honest, but not bragging or boastful because I feel that we in "rich" "free" America have our problems too. Lacking in wisdom is more a human quality. I did not want to tempt my fate with the Communist Government because I felt like I was tempting fate enough every time I rode in an automobile in China on their dangerous roads. But, you never hear about the "highway death toll" in China. When I asked about that sort of thing in my classes, I was told that information would make people unhappy. It also might get them to wear seat belts. I was the only person I saw in China who wore a seat belt. My drivers often acted insulted when I asked them to take it out of hiding for me to use.

Government Control of Housing

When a person gets a job in China they then become part of a Work Unit. Another powerful factor is that the Work Unit controls every person's living arrangements. Let me give an example from my university. All the university teachers and staff live in certain apartment buildings owned by the university. There are buildings for married staff, each unit having a living room, kitchen, two bedrooms and a bathroom. I was told that some how the couple can "buy" the apartment from the university, but if they leave they must sell it back to the university. The system never quite made sense to me, but it seemed great to them. It is like they paid rent, but got some money back, if ever they were to leave the university, which seldom happens.

The more flights up an apartment is located in China, the less expensive it is because there are no elevators in Chinese apartments. One English teacher, who I visited, lived on the seventh floor with no elevator. She was so proud because with the money she had saved walking so many steps she was able to buy her son a piano, which is a very expensive and high status item. There are also smaller studio apartments for single teachers, but even though some became my good friends, I was never invited to visit their apartments. I suspect that they were really small and not very nice.

Government Control of Marriage

The University Staff was highly encouraged to marry within the university community. Most of the teachers I knew were married to other teachers or administrators, etc. of the university. One of the weddings I attended was between two engineering teachers who were both in my class. The University President presided at the wedding, which was held in the ballroom of a local hotel. There is no sanction of religion in China, so hardly anyone would get married in a church. Another wedding I attended was held in the University Library where twelve couples, all on the University staff were married at the same time with hundreds of university students and staff present. Then the couples went to nearby hotels for their own private reception.

The Communist Party gives permission for a marriage. If a divorce happens, which is fairly seldom, the Communist Party first tries various types of pressure to keep the couple together. I know of only one divorced person who I met during my year in China. "For better or worse" are truly the vows that could be taken in China, meaning much more than they do in the US.

The Ultimate "Neighborhood Watch"

Many people and especially Communist Party Members seemed to keep tabs on others. I was shocked at the gossip and great interest the Chinese have for other people. It is like the "Ultimate Neighborhood Watch" program in the US, but everyone is watching everyone else and some are reporting to the authorities. I know that the name of any person who came to my apartment was recorded and sent to the Department of Foreign Affairs. People working in my apartment building entered my rooms on a daily basis. The outward purpose was to deliver hot water or to clean, but I know that they looked around my apartment in places that were not their business because I caught them on several occasions when I returned without their seeing me. They monitored every time I left and were so "friendly" to ask where I was going, if it was after class hours. The university always wanted me to have an escort if I left campus, except for near-by food shopping. They did buy a bicycle for me on World Women's Day and I rode a little off campus, but I considered streets to be very dangerous and I stayed close to the campus.

I was grateful for a watchful eye on me while in China, but I have no comprehension of a similar situation in the U.S.

A Whole Different World

I forgot to mention that our campus is walled-in, like most large companies and institutions in China. Apartment house complexes are also walled-in. My university has three gates with 24-hour guards. Now this did make me feel safe that only students and staff were allowed on campus. But, they also knew every time I left campus, the direction I was going, who I was with and what I carried with me. The university also knew that the beautiful flower gardens all over campus would not be disturbed, damaged or used as food by outsiders. There are definite advantages, but I don't know of any college or university that could be like that in the US. So many places in China, such as schools, hospitals and companies are walled-in with controlled access. It seems like a strange concept in the West, but very functional for many reasons including control of the large population and government control.

I heard that, once in a while, people can move to a single-family house that is privately owned. Each house is not walled-in, but the neighborhood of such houses does have a wall. One teacher who I got to know fairly well was going to move to a house close to the university after I left China. I never saw the house, but I saw a little village of houses being built near the university and she showed me the plans of one that was to be hers. The couple themselves did not have enough money to move out of their apartment, which I visited often, but the husband's parents were chipping in and three generations would live together. The grandmother would take care of her granddaughter, the couple's only child. The grandfather had to provide the maintenance for the house and then the teacher told me that she and her husband would be able to work longer hours for the university. Another teacher told me behind her back that this sounded so good except that the grandparents were very mean to the female English teacher, their daughter-in-law. I was told that they not only spoke in a cruel way to her, always being critical and disrespectful, but that they often struck her and she was made to serve them dinner without eating herself. These behaviors were typical in China's past, but do not seem to fit with modern educated people. She would be the last person in the family to eat and she only got what was left over, sometimes very little. The husband in the family was a university administrator and all adults in the family were members of the Communist Party.

I Experienced Control Through The Velvet Gloved Hands of My Students

I also was "under subtle control" while in China. I never went anywhere without the approval and a chaperone from the university. At first other university teachers escorted me around. After they knew me, that I wasn't up to something terrible, I could go with a university student. I was told that the students were talked to before they went with me and threatened to make sure I was safe and never left their sight. They also had to report back after our outing. The students always held on to me when I crossed a street. I didn't mind this because I felt better being taken care of. But, there can be a different point of view for their behavior. One vacation in the Spring I went to the home of one student for half the time and then to the home of another student for the remainder of the nine days. It was arranged that we would meet at a certain place to deliver me from one student to the next. I asked them if this was the changing of the "guards" or "baby-sitters?" They laughed and said, "Both." And then the one said that she was greatly relieved that her duty was over and had been successfully completed because she was worried what the university might have done to her if something had gone wrong.

The most "alone" thing I did while in China was to go to Beijing with a couple from Australia who also taught at the university. We were three adult foreigners traveling without an escort. But, the university made the plane and hotel reservations, took us to the airport and then there was a lady waiting at the hotel who monitored our daily activities. We could, of course, eat where we wanted to, but every morning she went over our plans, "in case we needed some help" and every night she was waiting for us to arrive at the hotel "to make sure that we had had a good time." She told us that she spoke regularly with officials from our university. At the time, I preferred to feel like I was being "cared for," but I think that other interpretations seem obvious. I did not have problems with the close supervision I experienced. I liked feeling safe and cared for and I wanted to get along well with the Chinese people and the university staff. I didn't have anything to hide and was willing to "fit with the program."

Now that I am away from China I realize things that I did not think of when I was there. Whenever Robert came to visit me he always brought me food that his wife had made. They decided that she was going to teach me how to cook Chinese food. I was a little interested, like I'm curious about everything, but I never had the idea of wanting "cooking lessons." Whenever I went to their apartment she did show me how to cook whatever we were eating and I was interested and listened. Robert would stop by my apartment frequently during the week to bring me samples of food and on the weekend I would go to their apartment to "learn to cook." I later realized that we could get together more often with this simple explanation for our frequent visits when actually we were mostly working on the material for this book. At the time, I didn't understand what was really going on.

The things that I'm telling you about the students aren't terrible. The control I experienced was not oppressive, but this is certainly not how things are done in free countries. We would not treat people like this in the US, either citizens or visitors. I would not want to live like these students and adults, and I feel sure that you agree.

Some people who I know enjoyed great benefits being part of the Chinese Communist Party. They had happy weddings, secure marriages and a few, private houses. Several of my adult university teacher-students were able to study abroad, but all, I found out, were party members and were greatly indebted to the Communist Government for every benefit they received. We all were "fitting with the program" and not "rocking the boat."

Living in Fear

That is where the fear comes in—"boat rockers" and sometimes even thinkers, don't do well in China, some do very poorly and some, as you will read about as you continue, are severely punished. Unfortunately, you will also hear about others who did not even live to tell their own stories.

Harry Wu describes the list better of those in jeopardy in China when he tells of his trip to "Xinjiang Uighur Autonomous Region (usually referred to as Xinjiang or Xinjiang Province) where they send our misfits, our outlaws, our dissidents, our class enemies, our thinkers, our questioners, our doubters, our dreamers, our scholars, our optimists, and our pessimists—anybody who thinks or feels—millions of us.... sprawling Xinjiang—land of thick, muddy rain, land of nuclear tests, land of prisoners working up to their waists in chemical vats—the badlands." (Wu, 1996, 7) It is also called Taklimakan which means "the bird can fly in but can never fly out." (Wu,1996,8)

I have to note that I wanted to go to this area while I was in China, but I was not allowed to go there.

I want to get started now on more interesting details on how I got to China, became adjusted to many cultural differences, started working, met Robert and then, most importantly, on to his amazing experiences and survival.

PART ONE:

JUNE GOES TO CHINA TO TEACH

Chapter One:

Leaving Colorado Springs

I had never been so nervous and excited in my life, not even on my wedding day or the days when I took my two Master's Exams. Then I remembered that this was actually most similar to how I felt the morning of the birth of my first baby, my daughter, after I had spent an entire night in labor, at home, basically alone. My very practical husband had slept all night. He said that there was no sense in both of us losing out on a night of sleep. So at about six a.m. when I finally woke him up to take me to the hospital, I was wired, fully charged and I WAS READY. That's how I felt this morning—READY—TO GIVE BIRTH—but this time to an adventure.

I had decided not to have my son (my second child) go to the airport with me because I was afraid that I would cry and carry on. It was my decision to go to China to teach, so there really wasn't anything to cry about. But just leaving my child, even though he was twenty-two years old, would bring tears to my eyes and questioning to my heart as to whether what I was doing was too selfish for a truly "good" mother.

I am basically an adventurous person. I had studied in Europe during college and had traveled to many different countries with my husband. I decided that a trip to China to teach for a year was my reward for twenty years of teaching in the US and successfully raising, pretty much by myself, two children. I could have cried very easily about almost anything because I was so nervous, excited, scarred, and apprehensive with the list of emotions continuing. This was one of the most daring things I had done in my entire life. I was literally going to live on the other side of the world to a country which has been fascinating to me since I was a child, but certainly isn't known for positive things like freedom or human rights. I wasn't planning on doing anything that would cause me trouble, so I wasn't worried, but on the other hand I didn't think much about potential problems that I could have. If I had thought too much, I might not have gone. It was best to just leave Colorado Springs, without fanfare, tears or an audience for any outbursts of the numerous emotions that I felt and could control much better alone.

So, I had asked a friend of mine to drop me off at the airport on her way to work at around 6:30AM. When I got there, the Colorado Springs airport was like an eerie nightmare. I had never imagined an airport so empty and quiet. I had arrived early enough that none of the bright lights were on nor ticket counters open and I assumed that only a very few airport employees were at work, somewhere, or at least the doors had been unlocked. The airport and city were small enough that there were no night flights in or out. The day was just getting started and there wasn't another person in sight.

As it turned out this was "the quiet before the storm." I'm glad that I enjoyed this time of peace to relax before my heart sped up again and stayed that way for most of the next twenty-six hours. I happily sat for a while at a row of attached chairs and relished the quiet and emptiness of a normally busy place. I don't think that I slept, but I was deeply relaxed and the time passed quickly.

After about one hour, the ticket counter opened. I decided that I did not want to be the first person to the counter, so I slowly dragged my two huge suitcases when I saw that another man would be in front of me. I tried to act like my suitcases didn't weigh as much as they did. I also had my laptop computer and a big carry-on bag. I must have been a funny sight, but fortunately no one was there to see it or make me feel self-conscious.

When it was my turn, the ticket man could barely lift the largest suitcase. Soon he said that it would cost an extra five hundred dollars for the additional weight. In disbelief I said that I couldn't afford that much. I then told him that "someone" had told me that they did not pay attention to weight on foreign flights. He said that to the contrary, this was where they most carefully monitored weight. I actually couldn't remember where I had gotten that piece of erroneous information, which I had never really thought much about, but just clung to in the hope of it being true. I very slowly and quietly choked out, "Well, what can I do? I'm going to live in China for over a year. That isn't a short vacation. I really need most of these things." He said that he would give me a box to fill with eighty pounds of the less important items that had to be left behind.

I was in shock and so thankful that this was the quiet Colorado Springs airport. There were by now less than ten people in sight as I causally dragged my luggage to a near-by "out of the way" corner of the terminal. I balanced the box on the row of attached chairs and spread out the two suitcases on the floor. I started; it seemed in slow motion, to look at each item I had packed and decide if I needed it or could live without it for twelve to eighteen months. I have no idea how I was making these determinations.

After a little time had passed, the ticket man appeared and said that he had thought of another idea. He asked if I could afford one hundred-thirty dollars for an additional suitcase. That sounded very reasonable to me and I was suddenly elated. But then I realized that I didn't know how I could get another suitcase. I started to explain that someone had dropped me off and I didn't know how I could get another suitcase. He said with a smile that he had damaged suitcases that people had left after insurance claims. He would pick out the one that was in the best shape. That sounded like the most wonderful idea. Basically, then I "just" had to repack the three suitcases to weigh about seventy pounds each. He reminded me that I also had to pick out about ten pounds of items to leave behind. While he went to get the damaged suitcase, I re-evaluated each item in the box by my new standards. I wish that there could be some way to replay my thoughts at a time like this. I wasn't sure if it now would seem outrageously funny or show an incredible emergency reserve of decision making ability or maybe both.

I have no idea how many people passed by me. I must have been an unusual sight. I think that some people thought that I was selling or giving things away from the open suitcases. Some people slowed and were looking at me very closely, but I had no time to care. I was packing, repacking and shuffling things around. I was glad that I had gotten to the airport early so that I could reasonably solve this problem. I could not believe hearing a first call for boarding for my flight. I left my suitcases open while I frantically found a phone to call my friend to come sometime that day to pick up the ten pounds of odd items that had been cut from my trip and left in a box at the ticket counter. I actually thought that I might never see any of those things again. I actually didn't care if someone took something from the open suitcases because that would just be one less item to be weighed. I closed and dragged my now, three suitcases to the ticket counter. I think that they still did not weigh in correctly, but the man didn't have the heart to say anything more. I put the one hundred-thirty dollar charge on my credit card, gave the man the jumbled box of rejected items and ran to the gate for the final boarding. I was the last person to board the plane. It was 9:30 AM, my hair was damp with sweat and I was now a combination of excited and exhausted, but I was on my way to China.

I sat next to a woman who quickly gave me some perspective on life and kept me quietly respectful. She was on her way to Minneapolis to sort through her parents' possessions of a lifetime. Her mother had died three years earlier and her father died two months ago. She talked of feeling like an orphan at the age of fifty. She finally felt able to go to the house where she had grown-up and sort through her parents' stuff. It made me feel like what I had just done was not that big of a deal. I was still so excited, but I thought that it might be good to just focus on someone else's life and problems for a while. I practiced being a good sympathetic listener and for now my problems seemed too small to talk about compared to hers.

Chapter Two:

Minneapolis to Tokyo

The flight to Minneapolis passed quickly and after my long conversation I felt a little calmer. Very quickly I boarded the 747 bound for Tokyo flying north over Canada and Alaska. I was in the middle section with no window to look out and the movies were terrible, so I took out a book and started reading about China. I really had had too much to do to get ready to go to China to have time to read much before today. I started getting in my mind a brief sketchy history because the actual one seemed very complex and so confusing. Here is my summary of the information I read:

*   *   *   *

June's Brief History of China—Part I

Separated from the rest of the Eurasian continent by great mountain ranges, wide deserts and open steppe, China's early contact with Europe and Western Asia was never more than marginal and sporadic. Until the nineteenth century, very few Chinese had visited Europe, and those travelers who came to China by land or by sea came primarily on trading missions and occasionally for small-scale settlement.

When China was part of the Mongol World Empire which stretched across central Asia, the Pope sent embassies from the Vatican to the Khan. And of course, the famous Marco Polo, the Venetian, had traveled to China, served as an official of the government and recorded his real and possibly some fictitious adventures for posterity.

For most of human history the great civilization of China had been the equal and superior of any contemporary culture in the world, but in the sixteenth and seventeenth century the Christian nations of the West obtained an advantage in various practical fields related to science.

During this period, fortunately for China, its isolation ended when educated Jesuits came as missionaries. But, more important to the country than the faith they taught was the knowledge of scientific techniques from Europe. Later, the energetic and aggressive Protestant missionaries were more successful with actually sharing religion with the common people by emphasizing personal salvation and Bible-reading.

But at the end of the eighteenth century another import to China was competing with religion and winning. Opium was first introduced as a medicinal drug, but without control it became increasingly popular as a narcotic. By the 1830's opium represented half the value of British imports into China. In a moral sense the trade was indefensible because the British had prohibited opium within their own territories. After 1839–1842, the time of the Opium War, China lost much to the British with the cession of Hong Kong, besides agreeing not to prohibit trade in opium in the future. Opium remained a problem until trade in it officially ended during the early years of the republic in 1917.

This first war with the European country of Great Britain and the treaties which followed established a pattern of relations between China and the West that lasted for the next hundred years. Very seldom was China able to mount a convincing or successful show of force, and each defeat that they suffered was followed by a dictated 'unequal' treaty that included indemnities in cash, transfers of territory and further privileges for foreigners.

Despite these times when China was forced to be weakened, the Empire during the nineteenth century was one of the greatest and most extensive in the world. It was rivaled in power and size only by the British Empire, which was not one land mass, but had parts spread around the globe. The other rival of China's greatness was the vast territory sweeping across Asia into Europe governed and better unified by the Russian Czars.

*   *   *   *

I certainly was headed for a place with a most amazing history. I could hardly take it in and in the future, I would read and reread about the history of China each time I needed to figure out the background for cultural incidents or unusual patterns of thought or other differences that I encountered. I most often found things from China's history that helped the present make sense.

After eating the first of three meals on this flight, the shades were drawn and it seemed most people were able to sleep. I was still too wired and so after a bit of reading, to get some exercise, I went to the back of the plane and lifted the curtain to look out the window. The sky was absolutely clear and sunny. Below us were mountains, it seemed like hundreds of them. It was like a magnificent sea of snow-capped mountains. I had never seen such beauty. But, there was one mountain that stood above the rest. I made an educated guess from having seen photos of it and said to the children who were also standing in the back of the plane that we were looking at Mt. McKinley, which was the highest peak in North America. The native name for it was Denali. It was absolutely breath taking. A stewardess heard me talking to the children and called the captain to verify my statement. I was thrilled that I had managed to come for a view at the best possible moment and was able to identify Mt. McKinley. Unfortunately my camera was packed away so that I could not get a photo. I just stayed and looked in wonder. It almost made the thirteen hours on the airplane worth it.

I must tell you about what I thought was a brilliant technique, besides reading, that I used to maintain my sanity on this thirteen-hour tortuous flight from Minneapolis to Tokyo. Whenever I needed a break, I would get in line to use one of the lavatories. I didn't actually take up time in the precious rest room because the lines were always long. Rather, I would constantly give people behind me skips so I could continue to stand up and move around a little rather than sit in the horribly cramped seats. I felt that I could stand in a line for about twenty minutes at a time without calling too much attention to what I was really doing. Then after I felt uncomfortable standing too long in the line for the lavatory at the back of the plane, I moved to the line for the lavatory in the middle of the plane.

Chapter Three:

Arriving in China

The third part of my flight was from Tokyo to Shanghai. After I had boarded the plane and got somewhat comfortable, I started thinking about my arrival in Shanghai. I suddenly realized that if the people from my university failed to meet me as they said they would, I did not know what I would do. I had no back-up plan and I had over two hundred ten pounds of luggage, no Chinese money, did not know how to say "hello" or "help" in the language and I was going to be arriving around 9:30 PM. I already was exhausted and my adrenaline seemed to be running out. I could be headed for disaster.

In the past, when I had felt such moments of panic I knew that the best thing is to just take one step at a time. As long as I had something constructive to do and I could keep moving forward, I would be OK. I knew that I really should save the panic for when I ran out of those two things. The step right now was to sit on the plane until it landed and then I would follow other people as I had in Tokyo. I would go where they went and do what they did. I could do that so there was no need for panic, yet. I was not able to relax because I started thinking of possible scenarios of what I could do if stranded in Shanghai. None of the scenes in my head looked very good.

Then I remembered seeing a man getting on the plane who looked like an American. I looked around for him, then gathered my nerve, went to where he was sitting and explained to him my potential problem. He seemed very experienced and knowledgeable. He simply stated that without question my Chinese university would be there as promised. He said that he had no doubt and he said this with such certainty that I couldn't argue except to say that if they didn't come; I would look for him for help and he smiled. I did feel better now knowing that I had a back-up plan, if I needed one.

When the plane landed, I slowly gathered my belongings and waited for others to disembark so I'd have a bigger group to follow. We walked and walked and walked. I always have a sense of humor so I was trying to figure out reasons for such a long walk. Maybe they wanted to give you plenty of time to enter China in case you wanted to change your mind and run back to the plane. Or maybe they only allowed the healthiest people to enter China and you had to prove your health and fitness with what seemed like a ten-mile hike.

But we soon divided up into lines to give someone the health questionnaire we had filled out on the plane. If our answers were satisfactory, I guess, assuming they could read English, we went on to the next line with our passports in hand. I tried to look friendly and sweet, but vulnerable enough that I might pass out if they even asked me a question. I just kept quiet and I kept moving. Some people were having difficulties, but my official did not even speak to me.

Soon I followed others to the next step, which was to get our luggage. People got a bit crazy at this point as if the first ones to find their suitcases would get a million-dollar prize. I was pushed, bumped and smashed into. I certainly wasn't going to get a prize because I could not find my suitcases any where. I kept going back and forth between the two monstrous luggage carousels for our flight, but nothing familiar came into sight. More and more people were gone from the area, but I still could not see my luggage. My heart was starting to sink as I stood there wondering what I should do. Then off in the distance moved to the middle of the empty first class carousel was a pile of the three suitcases that were mine. My thought was that since they weighed so much it was assumed they must be first class or maybe first class suitcases could weigh more and the man at the ticket counter had covered for me. Possibly the one hundred-thirty dollars allowed my luggage to fly first class, but that didn't include me. I was just so relieved, but my next problem was to get the three suitcases from the middle of the carousel. All of a sudden a good-sized man appeared and lifted each suitcase onto my flatbed cart. I don't know where he came from. I didn't even have time to ask him for help and as he was moving them, I said a quick "thank you." I then moved on to possibly the most difficult part and I was recharged.

I looked around at which direction people were taking now and headed that same way. Customs was next. What a nightmare, having to show a year's worth of possessions. I wasn't sure where I would begin. But the area was crowded and people were backed up and standing all over. We were in a huge building divided by a rope. I looked to the other side of the rope and there was a crowd of people waiting for passengers. There were many people holding signs, which I quickly and frantically scanned. Then I saw the most beautiful sign saying, "June Mudan" on the top line with the name of my university neatly printed beneath it. Tears came to my eyes and I yelled to the small group of people holding the sign and pointed to myself, "That's me, that's me!" Tears flooded down my face in such great relief. Yang, the adult of the group, motioned for me to keep going.

Yang later told me that she too was relieved when she saw me. She had worked so hard to get me to her university and then she worried about what I would be like. Would things work out or would I present more problems than I was worth? She would be the one to receive the credit or blame and that was a serious position to be in at a Chinese university. But she said that with my expression on my face and tears, she knew that I would be nice to work with.

The two young men who were with Yang quickly ran around the rope, grabbed my cart and pushed it around the crowd past the customs officials. No one stopped them and as they disappeared, I went around the rope and I gave Yang a big hug like she was a long-lost friend. But, to me it was more like collapsing in her arms. As the young men and my luggage disappeared, Yang could read my expression and said that I shouldn't worry because they were going to get the car from the university. She very proudly said that the university had provided a car and driver to pick up the American teacher. She told me that I was the first American teacher to live at the university. I was too tired to care about much of anything. I just followed along. I was so relieved to have successfully made it to this point and to have people there for me. It seemed like nothing else could be a problem or concern and I just wanted to get to my apartment and go to bed.

Chapter Four:

The Drive from Shanghai

I have always prided myself on either being content in the moment or being wise enough to appreciate a difficult situation knowing that at any time something worse could happen. I had thought that the worse thing was the thirteen-hour flight from Minneapolis to Tokyo. It was cramped, claustrophobic and after seeing the fabulous mountains, it seemed it would never end. There wasn't much good about it except that it was getting me to China.

After arriving in Shanghai, came what was probably the most dangerous and definitely the worst part of my journey. We had to drive several hours from the old Shanghai airport to where my university was located. I soon came to the conclusion that I had safely flown to China only to die in a car accident on my way from the airport. Most of the time, I was actually too tired to care. Every once in a while, though, something would come to my attention that caused me to get quite upset. I mostly thought of my poor daughter and son sacrificing their mom for a crazy adventure that had hardly begun.

We were on a toll-road like an American expressway, but the lanes seemed much narrower than the ones in the U.S. Trucks, but not ones like in the U.S., rather rickety old ones, loaded so full that they either seemed they would tip over or the boxes or whatever it was that was tied on would start to fall off right in our path. The trucks seemed to be going so slowly and we seemed to be passing every one of them going fast—too fast for safety. We passed everything and were weaving back and forth in the lanes like I had never seen anyone drive except maybe in a movie. The driver would brake behind a vehicle, flash his headlights, blow the horn and then take off passing it. It seemed that he did it without looking carefully for other traffic. Several times the driver actually wove in and out passing trucks in both lanes. He spent so much time blowing the horn at anything and everything. I tried to look at the speedometer and it seemed to point to about 80, but I wasn't sure if that was M.P.H. or K.P.H. I couldn't even think which speed was the faster. I was very anxious and kept making comments to Yang that I had been driving since I was fifteen or that I had been driving for almost forty years and had never imagined someone driving like this. I often questioned our safety. Yang once yelled at the driver and he yelled back at her as if that only added to the fun that he seemed to be having. She so sweetly assured me that, "He is the university driver." I wanted to say, "What does that mean? Does he have a Ph.D. in driving? So what, if we get killed." I kept saying that this was not safe and I was frightened. I actually asked more often—"How much longer?" than I had thought on my thirteen hour flight.

I was very tired and very frightened, but then I tried to be quiet for fear that I might get hysterical because I was also very cold. It was freezing cold because a back window in the van was wide-open and there either was no heater or it didn't work. I began to think longingly about the wonderful plane flight where at least I was warm.

Then, at last, I saw a huge dragon like on a billboard only bigger, freestanding and three-dimensional. I later used that dragon for the year to let me know that I was close to my university. We came to a quick turn and stop, and then a gate opened for us. In very dim lighting we drove across the empty campus because it was after midnight, but it seemed that we were driving on the sidewalk. At least we were going slowly and it was too late for students to be walking around.

I later found out much about driving in China. My ride from the airport was pretty typical of driving in China and it probably would have been more dangerous had the driver followed American driving laws. There seem to be few driving laws in China, not about speed, lane changing or using signals other than constantly blowing the horn. I later recorded with a movie camera a drive that I took each week from the university to the high school where I taught one day each week. I remember dreading the drive and giving a huge sigh of relief each time I survived it. I also found out that since so few cars ever entered the campus, when they occasionally did, the sidewalk was their road.

What a day!!! What a night!!! What next???

When we finally drove the four blocks and climbed a long stairway and then walked the very long hallway to my apartment and entered, it was freezing cold inside. There was absolutely no heat. Yang kept fooling with and mumbling about the "air-conditioning." I kept telling her that I don't need "air-condition-ing," I need *HEAT*. There was much I had to learn about China. She finally said she could do nothing until the morning and then left. I was devastated. I wanted to cry and go back home, but the only solution I could think of was to dive under the blanket with all my clothes on and pray that I would fall asleep fast, which I did.

CHAPTER FIVE:

MY FIRST WEEK IN CHINA

The next few days are a blur of adjusting my body clock to China time. The first time I woke up in my unheated apartment, it was still dark. I had my watch set to Colorado time and I could not focus enough to figure out the difference. I got up and to get warm, I started to unpack my suitcases and organize my possessions in the wonderful wall of cabinets and closets that lined my bedroom. This much space would normally be needed by an American at home, but I didn't have near enough belongs to start to fill it. I decided to take all the room I wanted to organize the things I had.

Yang had bought some food for me, including bananas, instant coffee and some packages of what she called "baby cookies." It turned out that I usually liked foods the Chinese had for their babies or children. After a short time, I went back to sleep, getting up every few hours to use the bathroom, eat something and/or unpack more of my things. I never had in my entire life so few items to organize in so much space, so I took great care and pleasure in organizing things like I never had before.

I could tell that the daylight of my first day had passed and it was getting dark. I got dressed for a visit from Yang. I was very surprised when it wasn't Yang knocking at my door, but the Director of the Foreign Language Teaching Section with a welcoming gift of famous Hangzhou tea. We had only spoken a few sentences when Yang arrived to take me out for dinner. I couldn't believe that she took me to an open-air restaurant for a big bowl of noodles with small pieces of chicken and, I think, spinach. I thought that this was crazy to be sitting outside. Didn't anyone in China like heat? Why would any person in their right mind sit outside and eat when it was so cold. I was freezing, but I appreciated having the warm food in my stomach. After we walked back to my apartment Yang was able to get the air-conditioner to produce a little heat. She tried to explain how it worked and what I needed to do. I didn't care. I just wanted to return to my great escape—my warm bed and sleep. She was barely out the door and I went right to bed and to sleep. I hoped that I would wake up in a warm American home and be amazed at my nightmare of freezing in China.

Also during that day I figured out the time difference between my watch and China. I made a chart for the times in the US because I had parents at Eastern Standard Time, a son at Mountain Time and my daughter at Pacific Time. I woke up around 1 AM and could not go back to sleep since it was daytime in the US. I decided to re-arrange the furniture in my two rooms. I wanted the bed closer to the heat source and chairs in the living room where people could sit and visit. I finally went back to sleep until two young teachers came in the morning to take me to the bank and post office.

The problem in the morning was that it was raining very hard and I was still so cold that I could not handle adding getting wet. I don't think that I actually had proper rain-gear for such a downpour. Rain like this in Colorado would have caused flash flooding and no one would go outside and walk around like they were planning. We waited for quite some time without a change in the rain intensity and we decided to cancel the trip. But, it was also their responsibility to get something for me to eat. They ordered Chinese fast-food delivery. That seemed pretty nice and so modern. As soon as they left, I had a nap until Yang arrived with dumplings for me for dinner. I appreciated it so much that I did not have to go out on such a cold and wet evening. I wondered how people ate in the rain in an open-air restaurant, but I did not want to find out.

The rest of the week was spent adjusting to the time change and recovering from the long stressful trip. I slept as much as possible, all night and often taking several naps during the day. When not sleeping I did whatever needed to be done to organize my possessions, make my apartment comfortable, set up my computer, printer and scanner and get myself otherwise ready to teach. I was in a learning mode, open for whatever I could learn to hopefully survive and possibly thrive in this very different culture and terribly cold place.

Chapter Six:

Learning about Life in China—The Most Difficult "Camping Trip" of my Life

I had no idea when I left the U.S. what an adventure and challenge it would be living in such a different culture. There was so much to learn about China; basic life skills, the customs, proper etiquette and right now, most importantly, how to make it through the winter without getting sick because of the cold. The predominant feeling I had my first month in China was being cold, *VERY COLD*. The only place that I could thaw out was in my bed. I had the most wonderful blanket that I had ever seen that wasn't electric. I don't know what it was made from, but it reminded me of an old horsehair blanket that my grandmother had. It was heavy but without the great weight of horsehair. The ladies who took care of my apartment were in disbelief when I asked to have an additional blanket like that. They told someone to translate to me that "one is enough; there was only one for each bed." I later told Yang that I wanted; rather NEEDED an additional blanket, and soon they brought the extra blanket with a smile for the "spoiled" "weak" American. I thought I could tell their thoughts by the looks on their faces, without needing a translator. Some expressions, I think, are human nature anywhere in the world. Their faces said to me, "We may have lost having to give you the extra blanket, but, you're the sissy." Yang conferred that I was right about the meaning of their expressions.

I was very lucky that Yang had experienced living in a foreign culture. She had, as a college student studied for one year in Australia. She also had traveled to the United States, one time, for about two weeks with a delegation from the university.

She acted as their own interpreter who they could trust, in addition to the ones provided by the universities they had visited. She had a good understanding of living as a "foreigner" in a strange land and she had some ideas about what life was like in America. She knew that I was willingly sacrificing many comforts of my home to live in China and she in turn wanted to do whatever was possible to keep me satisfied and positive about my experiences. I felt very fortunate to have some one, not only experienced, but also understanding and caring like my wonderful Yang. I called that name as if it were her first name, but I think it was her last name. Chinese names can be confusing.

Yang and I had a rather long conversation about my being so cold. She, first, sternly said that she had very explicitly e-mailed me about bringing the warmest clothes that I had. I told her that I had done as she had said. She had not been in the U.S. in winter, so I tried to explain that in the U.S., every place is heated: homes, apartments, classrooms, cafeterias, restaurants, stores and especially our cars. The only time we are without heat is when we walk from our house to our car, until the engine gets hot or when we walk from our car to a classroom or a store which are all wonderfully warm.

I explained that in the U.S. we might go for a walk in the cold, play outdoors, some people even ski for hours, but when a person gets cold, we can very easily go to numerous places that are kept at about seventy degrees. My apartment in China, at its warmest, was around fifty degrees. I explained that under normal conditions, people in the U.S. do not live in such cold temperatures for a prolonged period of time.

There was no where for me to get warm except in my bed and in my "new invention" that I called a "June-warmer." The university had been very proud to have a small automatic washing machine for me in my bathroom. And in my living room was an electric clothes dryer on tall legs so that, theoretically, it could stand above the washer. I asked why it was in the living room and not in the bathroom and I got two answers. First, they said that they thought it might "not be good" to put it in my bathroom. It is very hard to explain what my bathroom in China was like, but I will try to describe my entire apartment which included two large rooms and two small rooms.

I will have to go into rather complicated details for you to understand how unusual things were set up and how creative I had to be to complete normally simple tasks in the U.S. You will soon understand why I call my time in China, "the most difficult camping trip of my life."

Probably the most important factor about life in China is that I could drink only bottled water. Tap water was totally unsafe for me, although the locals drank it all the time. I have to digress and add the gross detail that I came to the conclusion that the normal state of bowel movements in China seemed to be diarrhea. You may wonder how I got that awful idea and I maybe shouldn't tell you because I can't think of a nice way to put it. It relates to China's reputation of having the worst toilets in the world, often with piles of excrement within sight. I think that may be more information than you wanted to have, but that was part of life in China. Most American outhouses at campgrounds are far more pleasant than the typical Chinese facility. Many I wouldn't call "toilets" because they were pits that you straddled. I certainly would not call them "restrooms" because you ran in and out as fast as you possibly could, gagging until you reached fresh air. So, let's say they were the "location for bodily functions." Sorry for bringing it up! It was a fact of life in China. End of topic!

Back to my apartment! I had a large tank of drinking water in my apartment without which I would not have survived. The water was either room temperature or if I pressed a button, a small amount was heated. A corner of my living room I designated as my kitchen which had a small table, a small refrigerator and a microwave for cooking. The water tank was on the kitchen table. Also twice a day two large thermos bottles of boiling hot water were delivered to my apartment which also provided a nice opportunity for the ladies to check on "how" or what the American was doing. They were polite and curious when I was there and I'm sure more than snoopy when I wasn't.

There was an alcove off the living room that I called my "sink room" which had the only sink in my apartment that I used as both a kitchen and bathroom sink. From there you enter the bathroom that had the washing machine, a simple Western style toilet with a seat (lucky me!!!) and an old dirty-looking bathtub with a shower head and several extra faucet handles and other knobs. I insisted that the tub be scrubbed and then I cleaned it again myself before I would use it. It had a permanent ring that no amount of scrubbing for one year could remove. The bathroom tiles also looked dirty and never improved either. There also was a space heater attached to one wall and a hot water heater attached to the opposite wall near the bathtub faucet and showerhead.

My first three to four months in China I took a bath about once a week. I couldn't take a shower because only very hot water came out of the faucet with no cool water to mix with it. I didn't know what to do with only close to boiling water, so I would run a tub of it after dinner and I went into the bathroom every ten minutes or so until I thought it had gotten cool enough to get into. Sometimes, it took two hours to cool off enough for me to bathe. I also needed to wash my hair and use American hair color once a month, in the bathtub. I rinsed my hair by either dunking my head under the water or I later bought a small plastic waste basket which I filled and refilled with bath water that I poured over my head. I decided that I didn't think my hair was being rinsed well enough with the soapy bathwater so I bought two additional plastic buckets that I filled with hot water and then took them to the sink room. I used a glass to add cold water until I thought the temperature was tolerable. Since both the water from the sink and bathtub was not for drinking I always had to be very careful to not get it in my mouth when I poured it over my head or put my head under water.

It took me months and finally help from students to figure out how to use the rusty shower handles and how to get the nozzle to produce water of a comfortable temperature. For some reason, I did not feel like asking Yang for help with this problem. It seemed embarrassing and I wanted to save her for the bigger problems. After I became friends with a few Chinese students I asked a girlfriend and boyfriend who were visiting me at the same time to help me figure it out. I was immediately asked by them with total puzzlement; don't you have showers in America? I said that we did, but they were nothing like this Chinese shower and I didn't feel like describing what the differences were. I was afraid I'd become insulting comparing this situation to the clean modern convenient bathrooms I had in America. Until I went to China, I too would have assumed that a shower is a shower or a toilet is a toilet, the same all over the world. There also was no shower curtain or a rod to put one and no one seemed to know what I meant. When I finally learned how to use the shower my whole bathroom got wet, which didn't matter because there was a drain in the floor and that is where both the bathtub and washer drained into. The frame around the bathtub had a hole for the water to drain on the floor. Trying to be positive, I looked at this as a way of killing two birds with one stone, so that every time I took a bath, showered or did laundry my bathroom floor got washed. I soon bought a special plastic container to hold the toilet paper which got wet when I showered. The T.P. was not in a roll, but a pile like small rough tissues.

Such a set-up with water running on the floor was not a good place to have an electric clothes dryer. With the way things were, I was careful whenever I used the bathroom. When doing laundry I moved the washer close to the door so that I didn't actually stand in the bathroom when loading or unloading clothes. Where I stood was dry and I plugged the washer into a living room outlet. Believe me that I also was very careful about touching the electric heater and water heater if the floor was wet. All of this was not only inconvenient, but I also thought, dangerous. I tried to explain the danger to the apartment manager and he could not understand what the problem was. For some reason it was bad to have the electric clothes dryer in the bathroom, but the electric washing machine, heater and water heater were OK? I decided that they wouldn't want to kill their first American teacher, so it must be safe. There were many things about China that I did not understand and I would put these items on the list.

You might ask how the Chinese take baths or showers. Most of the teachers had similar bathtubs in their apartments, but to my knowledge they weren't used for bathing. Once I had to use the toilet in a teacher's apartment and there was no light bulb in her bathroom. She said that I shouldn't become frightened if I heard a splash in the bathtub because the fish they were having for dinner was swimming in the tub until it was time to kill and cook it. The Chinese have a reputation for liking fresh food and I could go into many stories about that. I feel that I am digressing from my digressions. Most Chinese went to bath houses located on the streets around the university. There also was a bath house on campus for the students. It cost money to use it so many students never did. Instead, I was told by the boys that they usually took cold showers in their cold dorms. They were such hardy young people.

One time when I was having difficulty with water, I asked Yang about the bathhouse on campus and she almost had a stroke. She said "NO!!" so emphatically. She said that all the girls run around naked and I would have to be naked and they would all stare at me. She asked me how I felt when people on the street stared at me. (It didn't bother me that much.) Then she said that the entire bathhouse would come to a halt for everyone to look at me. I asked if there were no private areas or private showers. I could tell that she was upset and didn't even understand what I meant. I became embarrassed because this was becoming a much bigger issue than I meant it to be. I dropped the subject, never to mention again until now.

Before I finish the topic of water use in China, I have to tell you what reminded me the most of camping. It was the complex operation of washing dishes. The good part was that there was American antibacterial dish soap available at my local food store. I used large quantities of it for washing the dishes, my hands, my body and anything else that needed washing. There were many steps to washing dishes. First, I used the sink water to rinse a dish, but that water was not for drinking and was air temperature so it never cut the grease. Next, I rinsed with the thermos of boiling water. Then I put the antibacterial soap on the dish and rubbed it around. Then I had a small bucket that I used just for rinsing dishes. Since I used so much soap and the rinse water became soapy quickly, I also did a final rinse with the boiling water from the thermos. As you can probably picture, the water and the dishes were very hot and I often burned my fingers. It was strange though, how the intense heat on my fingers didn't seem as bad because the rest of me was so cold. Maybe my blood in my fingers got heated and warmed the rest of my body. I usually liked washing dishes because it made me feel so warm. You might think of other ways I could have washed the dishes, but another factor was that there was not a lot of space at the sink or on the small kitchen table.

I have to add one more interesting detail about living in a foreign country that has its own kind of eating utensil. Everyone was amazed at how quickly and well I learned to use chop sticks. My clever answer was that I was evidence of "survival of the fittest." I like to show off, so at one birthday party I was invited to, I fed each of the six boys at the table one peanut which I carefully picked out of a bowl, carried across the table and dropped into the boy's mouth. I had lots of fun in every way I could.

Back to my apartment, I had chop sticks and cheap metal forks, spoons and knives. One might think that in the privacy of my apartment I would only use the American utensils, but I didn't, and I didn't realize what I was doing until one of the teachers asked me about it. If I was eating food that was Chinese in form, I grabbed the chopsticks. If I had made food that was certainly American to me, I used a fork and knife. This really made sense. Most Chinese food is already cut into small pieces and grabbing those pieces is easy to do with chop sticks. Most American food is whole or in large pieces, so a knife and fork are needed. Most of the Chinese students used big spoons to eat. Sitting around the cafeteria on shelves, window sills or wherever there was a spot were hundreds of what we would call serving bowls with one big spoon. Each student had their own bowl and spoon; they were responsible for rinsing it clean after each meal and finding a place to store it until the next meal. This certainly saved the university a great expense of washing and sanitizing dishes. It wasn't a bad idea when it was cold, but I think when there were flies, it was very unhealthy. There also was only cold water to rinse the bowls.

The student cafeteria actually had two different operations. The bottom floor had cheap common food that most of the students ate most of the time. It cost pennies. The second floor was where teachers, guests and students could eat, but the food was more expensive like about $1.25 to $2.00 per meal. One day I said that I wanted to try a student meal and I was told "absolutely no." They would refuse to serve me. I tried to explain that I was meaning no harm, but was just curious. They told me that Confucius had a story about curiosity killing a cat. I didn't know that was his idea.

Getting back to why the clothes dryer was in the living room, the other answer I was given is that it was a real status item. Hardly anyone had seen one and whenever I had guests to my apartment, after taking off their shoes, the first thing they did was to examine it. One day when showing it to someone it dawned on me that I could briefly run the dryer and put my upper body inside to warm up. The metal actually got so hot that I had to lean on a big bath towel. It certainly got warmer than either of the "air-conditioners" in my living room or bedroom. I think that this shows how desperate I was to get warm.

I was worried that I could not stay healthy when constantly cold. I was also concerned that I might get irritable and crabby. Bone chilling cold does not foster feelings of well being, health or kindness. I wondered what could be done to help me make my life more tolerable.

Yang and I seemed to communicate quite well from the beginning. I didn't whine and complain, but rather simply told her what the problem was and asked her for possible solutions. I felt like when I had a problem I was always in a problem-solving mode. If necessary I was willing to do whatever needed to be done to solve the problem, but being in such a different environment I often did not know the best solution and had to ask my experienced Chinese person, Yang.

Yang said that we would go shopping in a few days when the stores were open and get some warm Chinese clothing. But, for now, she invited me to her apartment for a very special dinner the night of the Spring Festival Holiday. I wasn't interested in the food or the holiday, but was happily thinking that I would have an evening of being warm at her house.

Yang came to my apartment to get me in the late afternoon. First we walked to a food store where I could pick out things that I wanted to eat, since the food she had bought for me on my arrival to China was running out. The first time being in a Chinese "super market" was amazing. I could have looked around for hours. I'm not sure what I was most excited about, the American foods that I recognized or the strange items that I had no idea what they were. There were many American products such as M & M's, Oreo Cookies which said on the package,

"America's favorite cookie," instant coffee, pistachio nuts from California and frozen American sweet corn with an American flag on the plastic bag. What was totally missing and something I went without for the entire year was butter. When I got homesick, I often ate American sweet corn and mashed potatoes mixed together, with the yellow from the corn tricking me into believing I had butter.

The climb to Yang's apartment or condo gave me sufficient exercise for the day. We had to climb to the seventh floor since there wasn't an elevator and she said that few buildings in China, with less than eight floors, had elevators. She laughed at how when she was in America, people took the elevator from the first to the second floor. I asked her about the concept in America that apartments on the top floors are more expensive because of the view. She said that it was opposite in China, that the higher the floor, the less expensive the apartment because of the greater climb. Then she got a big smile on her face when she told me that soon I would see what she had bought with the money she saved by living so high up.

When I got inside her apartment and it was just as cold as the outside air, I knew there certainly wasn't a heater or furnace in her house. She explained that what is used in China is called an air-conditioner and it is a combination heater in the winter and air conditioner for the summer. She said though, that it cost about one year's salary. She explained that if you've always lived in the same temperature as the outdoors, you get used to it. I wondered how long that might take, but it turns out that she was correct. After my year in China my house in America is much cooler than the temperature most Americans keep. I'm not saying that I prefer the fifty degrees like I had in my apartment, but seventy degrees or more is now too warm for the "Chinese girl" that I have become.

Then finally she got to show me what she was so proud of—the piano that she had bought for her son. She told me that pianos in China are very expensive. Her seven-year-old son played several songs for me while Yang and her husband excused themselves to go into the kitchen to prepare dinner.

Then her son "entertained" me more with fireworks. I think he had been told he had to play so many songs before we could do the fireworks. We did spend time shooting off more fireworks from their seventh floor apartment window than I had in my entire life in the U.S. I could not believe how cheap and common fireworks are and when I spoke of dangers, they looked at me like they had no idea what I was talking about. I explained that there are laws in America that relate to personal safety and the fire hazards involved in the use of fireworks. I tried to tell how usually a city would buy a large supply of really fabulous fireworks for everyone to enjoy together in the park. Yang's husband said that he thought we were free to do anything we wanted to in America. He did not understand laws restricting fireworks use. I could tell that he thought that what I was saying was so strange and totally different from what he had ever imagined about life in America.

Later, I found out how news coverage in China is government-controlled and very different from what I was used to. People aren't told about unpleasant things in China. People do not read about the number of kids who blow their fingers off or start their clothes on fire with the cheap, easily available and often defective fireworks. They may hear about one child in their own neighborhood, but such news and statistics aren't made known like in the U.S. People could hardly believe me and could not understand what I meant when I said that fireworks are illegal in most American cities. I was told that Americans are free to do anything, so why couldn't they get any fireworks that they wanted.

The same news restrictions apply to driving safety in China. After seeing the insane driving habits, I asked my students about accident and death statistics. No one in my classes had any information. They almost didn't understand what I meant. One student said that the government probably thinks that it would only make people unhappy. One of the greatest differences I experienced while in China is a lack of the concept of "truth." I think that due to a need for survival, the Chinese have developed a practice of telling what they think you want to hear and not necessarily what is the "truth." I had not remembered that "ignorance is bliss" is an old Chinese proverb. But, it was something I would think about a lot later.

When at Yang's apartment, I mostly wanted to be in the kitchen partly to see how the food was being prepared but mostly to stand beside the big propane stove burners that provided such wonderful heat. They finally allowed me to go into the kitchen with them, but they said only because I was an American. They said that Chinese guests would wait in the living room until the food was prepared. Let me say that very little they made looked like the food we get at Chinese restaurants in the U.S. I never ceased to be surprised how different the food was. Most food in China was very flavorful and delicious but also quite time consuming to prepare. There were only a few foods that I was unwilling to try—duck blood soup and chicken feet topped that list.

When we sat down at the table, there were more than twenty bowls and plates with various kinds of Chinese "dishes." There were several types of meat, fish and the "shrimpiest" shrimp I had ever seen. Using my fingers, I tore off the head, tail and shell and felt there was hardly enough left to chew. Then Yang gave me a lesson in the Chinese way to eat shrimp. You put the whole little shrimp in your mouth and turn it around to bite off the head and spit it out. Then you turn it around again in your mouth and bite off the tail and spit it out. Then with your tongue and teeth you remove the shell and spit it out. Then you swallow the little morsel that is left. Eating shrimp like that reminded me of eating celery in that you burn more calories in the process of eating than you get from the food. I finally said that I am not so patient, but actually I could not really taste the little morsel that was left for me to eat. They said that they had gotten the shrimp especially for me, but since I didn't like them, they would gladly eat them.

Yang and her husband were so kind and sensitive during the meal in that when they noticed a food that I liked and went back to more frequently, they moved the bowl in front of me and they ate the foods that I liked the least. I explained that I finally understood that night, the set of Chinese dishes that my mother had bought for me. Her neighbor in Florida had lived in China for over twenty years, working for the American Embassy in Beijing. Since she was getting old and was moving into a retirement home, she sold many of her possessions. I was so pleased to get her set of Chinese dishes that she had brought back from Beijing. Tonight the lack of dinner plates and the abundance of little bowls and plates finally made sense to me. What I thought were dinner plates actually were serving plates along with the many serving bowls. There were so many little bowls and little plates that I wasn't sure how they could be used. Tonight I finally saw how the pieces were to be used. Each person had in front of them a small bowl and/or plate to put shrimp heads, tails and shells and what ever else you did not eat. When the little bowl or plate was full, it was taken away and replaced with a clean one. Most of the time the food went directly from the serving bowls using chopsticks into your mouth. I was told that it was not proper to have a knife at the dinner table because it is considered a weapon. Chinese food is all cut up in bite-sized pieces to just grab with chopsticks. It is amazing how the customs of other people make perfect sense when you find out what they have in mind.

One thing that I never got used to was that I never knew how much I was eating at each meal. I was accustomed in America to filling a dinner plate, sometimes to over flowing and maybe two times for a special dinner. I always "cleaned my plate due to the starving children in China" that I had heard of, as a child, in the 1950s. When everyone eats out of the same serving bowls and plates and the food goes right into your mouth, you have no idea how much you are eating. The concept is to eat until you are satisfied and leave the rest for the others. I usually ate until I was stuffed. I think that I actually ate more with the Chinese system.

I also did not know that the typical Chinese white or stir-fried rice would be served at the end of the meal. I was then too full to want any. That was the idea that at a banquet, you only ate rice if the other food did not fill you. I really liked having rice as I was eating other food because it seemed to calm the various strong spices that were in some dishes. I often asked if I could have rice during the meal and I'm not really sure what the Chinese thought of that. I felt that some people looked at me with disapproval. It didn't really bother me because I certainly had no thought of trying to please 1.3 billion Chinese people. No one ever joined me in eating rice throughout the meal and sometimes I think they thought that I was very strange and certainly not properly brought-up in America. Much later I learned that many meals in China just consisted of white rice. That was the most common every-day food often eaten several times a day. I always was served a banquet as a special guest from America. Many mornings in homes all over China, rice was all that was eaten and again the same for dinner except perhaps with some cooked greens. It was simple to make and a very easy way to save money. I can understand why Chinese might not want to eat rice at a banquet when there were so many other delicious dishes.

Chapter Seven:

Learning about Life in China—Shopping

Two days after Spring Festival Yang picked me up at my apartment and took me to the campus cafeteria for lunch. She then gave me a "Golden Dragon" Card with one hundred yuan credit. I could use it for any meal at the second floor cafeteria and I could add more money to it whenever needed. The university was very proud of this new system because it was a great way for students and staff to pay for their food without having to carry around and count out small amounts of Chinese money for the relatively cheap (but mostly quite delicious) food served by the university.

After that, we rode a very crowded bus to the downtown. The bus cost one yuan or about twelve cents. It was unbelievably crowded. When I say crowded, it was not like anything I had ever experienced. Crowded in China is not like crowded in the rest of the world. I could not believe all the people and all the traffic. There were many cars, buses and trucks, but mostly we saw bicycles, scooters, bike-wagons, scooter-wagons and moving contraptions of all sorts with everyone blowing their horns at each other.

We first went to the bank to cash one hundred dollars in travelers' checks. I was surprised how confusing the Bank of China was and apparently Yang was not a regular customer at a bank. University teachers were paid once a month in cash at the department office by the department chairman, so there was no reason to use a bank. Nothing seemed clear. We stood in one line and when we got to the window we were told it was the wrong line. When we went to the correct line and window we turned in the travelers' check, my passport and a written request for the money. Then we had to go to another line and window to actually receive the cash. All the while we were standing in lines men approached us speaking to Yang and telling her that they could give us a better rate of exchange. I could not believe it when she told me that the "Black Market" was working right inside the Bank of China.

Then we went across the street to a huge department store. Its size was impressive. We walked through so many different departments. Then we went up a huge staircase to the second floor where there was clothing. There must have been hundreds of sweaters of all kinds on wire models high above the cabinets that were loaded with sweaters in sealed plastic for people to purchase. The idea is that a person walks around looking over-head quite a distance away at the sweaters. There wasn't any way you could touch them. I was puzzled because the sweaters were not very colorful. They were mostly in shades of light brown or grey. Then Yang made a confession that we were in the men's department because the women's sizes were too small for me. I looked at her in disbelief, so we went to the women's department for me to see for myself. It was quite an unpleasant "reality check" for me to need a man's sweater and later I would learn that I needed the largest size they had.

The many clerks were not really helpful. Most of them just stood around apparently doing nothing. I later realized that they were there to keep an eye on shoppers. A few clerks who actually did the selling were quite aggressive following us around and saying things to Yang in Chinese which I was probably better off not understanding. They certainly did not like the idea that I wanted to look at a few sweaters close up. Apparently no other person had ever made such a request. They got a ladder and climbed up to remove the wire models and bring them down for me to see and touch. I really didn't mean to be so much trouble, but I was buying one sweater that I would be wearing almost everyday for perhaps two months until the weather warmed. I could not imagine wearing something without knowing what it felt like. This whole way of shopping seemed so strange to me. I finally decided on a sweater made of yak hair that would be very warm. Then we didn't know what size to get. I finally just decided to get the largest size. It turned out to be a good choice because it not only fit me and kept me warm, but now my daughter wears it as one of her favorites. It does fit her better than it fit me, but I always wore at least one layer of turtle neck shirt under it and sometimes when it was really cold, I wore two turtle necks.

When we were ready to make the purchase we were not allowed to take the merchandise. The clerk wrote out a ticket saying what we wanted and the cost, which we then took to the cash register. I had selected the most expensive sweater in the store that was two hundred-thirty yuan or about twenty-eight dollars and seventy-five cents. After we paid, another clerk wrote out another ticket saying we could be given the sweater because it had been paid for. I was starting to learn about one of the difficulties in China of having 1.3 billion people, most needing employment. I would also later learn that many people have the attitude that if something can be taken without paying for it, it's OK, if you don't get caught. Every effort needed to be made to prevent shop lifting and to employ the most people, all receiving a very small wage. There were so many differences for me to be learning.

Next we found yak hair long underwear which again we bought in the largest men's size at one hundred seventeen yuan or about fourteen dollars and fifty cents. This shopping was about all my ego could take for the day. But then we next looked at dishes, which is my favorite thing to shop for. I looked at every kind of dishes they had from the cheapest to the best. Yang was puzzled by the great care I took in shopping and deciding what was right for me. She thought I could just grab a few dishes and go, but I looked at every pattern and every option from expensive sets to the very cheapest individual pieces. Cost was not my main concern. I wanted something special and unique. She did not understand my reasoning and great deliberation. I'm not sure I knew what I was looking for, but I thought I'd recognize what I wanted when I saw it. Finally I made my choice of two flat bowls which were sort of like plates, but with high sides. I had never seen bowls shaped quite like that. Then I got two more typical serving bowls and Chinese spoons. All the pieces were decorated with the same unusual flowers in orange and light purple. The design was very nice. I bought two of each shape thinking that I might have someone over for dinner and I'd have a matching set. As it turned out, one time I had a total of four people over and we each had something to eat out of. I also bought a covered dish for cooking in the microwave which was my only method for cooking. In addition, I bought six tea cups in case I had guests for tea and America's favorite, Oreo cookies. It seemed fun to me to have a few versatile dishes and the total cost was about eight dollars and fifty cents. The microwave cooking dish was about two dollars and twenty-five cents.

I was exhausted from the cold and the shopping. Yang kindly offered for us to take a taxi back to the University, but I wanted to be "tough," so we took the crowded bus. It had been a very tiring full day and I was happy to be home knowing that with my new clothes I would be warmer and more comfortable. For now, bed was still my favorite place.

Chapter Eight:

I Begin Teaching

I had been in China for one week before I started teaching. My first class was held in the evening. The students who had enough money to leave for Spring Festival had not returned to campus and regular university classes were not in session. But, two nights each week I had been asked to teach the university teachers Spoken English. Most of the teachers had stayed in town for the holiday, so we could hold class. I felt that there were some high expectations of me to be teaching the teachers, but I also felt honored and very excited to meet the challenge. I looked forward to having a peer group to not just teach, but to learn from.

The head of the Engineering Department had selected about twenty teachers who were most likely to go over-seas to be in the class. I later found out that three of them were already scheduled to go to Europe to study in the fall and the class would be especially helpful for them. Most of the teachers had studied English for at least ten years. They could read it very well, having an excellent vocabulary. They could also write well, knowing grammar probably better than I did. But, they, like so many students in China could not speak English very well.

I later found out that this relates to two very specific problems with being Chinese. First, there are sounds in the English language that are not made in Chinese and these strange sounds were very difficult for the Chinese to learn. Of course, there are many more sounds that are in Chinese that are not in English and they seemed even stranger and harder for me to learn. Before I had left China I must have been corrected thousands of times and still am, each time I try certain sounds. There is just nothing to attach or connect these sounds to in English. Fortunately, my students did better with English sounds than I did with Chinese.

The biggest problem of all has to do with the Chinese culture. The people are so shy. They seem to have little confidence and were afraid to speak and make a mistake. If they said something wrong they might "lose face" which, was apparently a fate worse than death. I had so much fun dealing with this problem because I thought it was so silly. I had been raised as a very fearful child and I have been on a crusade my whole life to overcome my fears and, of course, to help others to over-come their fears. To me, saying something wrong seemed like a small mistake to make. My greatest fun was modeling for them how to make a mistake and laugh about it. They loved to hear about my latest lesson in the Chinese language and all the mistakes that I made. I, so often, said that the only failure was in not trying. My guess is that for some reason Confucius never thought of that. If he had, the whole country might be more willing to take risks and would have turned out less docile. Too bad for China!

I soon discovered that the American President, Bill Clinton, was the best role model of all for the Chinese. These people absolutely loved talking about him because they could not comprehend why he had not resigned as soon as embarrassing allegations were made. According to the Chinese, he had lost so much face with the detailed descriptions of his sexual behavior that he should have died of embarrassment on the spot. He actually taught them the best lesson. Not only did he survive the personal embarrassment, but he remained the President of our great country. He and his family experienced a difficult time which the people of China would never get to see their leaders experience. He showed the world that "losing face" would not kill you and not only could you survive, but eventually live to overcome the embarrassment and difficulties. He had survived and they could survive too, making some small speaking errors and then learning from them.

One of the techniques that I wanted to use to teach spoken English was teaching them to sing songs in English. When I was about twenty-five years old I had worked at a mission in Mexico. I now could speak few words in Spanish, but I can perfectly sing the songs we had sung with the Mexican children. My memory of those songs was flawless and I could apply the vocabulary from those songs to actually remembering many Spanish words.

So on our first night of class toward the end, we sang along with Kenny Rogers, "You Light Up My Life." I would not say it went over well. We had to sing it several times before they got all the words, even though I had printed a copy for each person and read the song first out-loud several times and explained the meaning of certain words. Most of the men were too dignified to sing along, but many enjoyed it. It got their mouths open and forced them to voice words in English with some volume and fluency. I just wish that I could have tried out my teaching ideas on the regular college students first rather than having this group of university teachers as my so to speak—guinea pigs.

There was an adult student in the class whose English name was Martin and who had the responsibility each evening of coming to my apartment and walking me to class and then returning me safely home after class. He was one of the teachers who was scheduled to go to Europe the next two years to work on a degree and then return to the university to teach. When he walked me home he was very encouraging of how class had gone. I had printed out an information sheet telling about myself: my education, my experiences, my family and some of my interests. I had gone over it in class as a way of introducing myself. The teachers were to use it as a model for the next class when they each had an opportunity to introduce themselves. He thought that it was a good assignment. He liked the singing. He was a fairly positive person. I later found out that he was a Communist leader on campus and he taught me many things that I did not know about Communism in practice in China.

The next day shortly after I had eaten lunch I came down with a full-blown head cold. It came on so rapidly that I could hardly believe it. I was fine when I was eating my lunch in the cafeteria and then walked over to the English department to send some e-mail. At the computer I suddenly started sneezing like I was allergic to something, but I also became instantly congested. Within minutes I went from feeling fine to having a miserable head cold. I went back to my apartment to drink lots of water, take vitamin C and take some of the cold medicine that I had successfully used in the U.S. and had brought with me. On Thursday I stayed home all day to rest up and try to get my cold under control before class at 7:00 PM. It was strange because the cold medicine had worked perfectly for me in the past and now it seemed to do absolutely nothing. Yang said that we could cancel the class, but I said that I'm not going to cancel my second class in China.

The class went pretty well. The teachers each had a presentation to make so I didn't have to do much talking. Not everyone showed up because many did not want to have to speak in front of the class. I do not remember much what each person said because I was not feeling well. There was one man who made a special impression on me. Most of the teachers were in their twenties or thirties, the oldest in his early forties. This man was much older, like in his seventies and he said that he was retired from teaching. He had a young girl with him who he introduced to me as his daughter. She looked about 15. He must have married or had a child quite late in life. His English was much better than the other teachers' English. He seemed more formal and proper, but yet very kind and warm-hearted. I was hoping that I would get to talk with him more because he seemed interesting.

One of the teachers had gotten speakers for my computer and that made the singing sound better tonight. I made the comment that my American cold medicine did not seem to be working and everyone laughed and agreed that was because I had a Chinese cold. When my Chinese teacher/escort walked me home he asked if I was going to go to bed immediately. I said that I thought I might watch the news in English, which came on between 10:00 and 10:30. About fifteen minutes later there was a knock on my door. He gave me Chinese medicine for my Chinese cold. I didn't take it that night. I wasn't convinced that there was such a difference. But, after my second day of suffering as if I wasn't doing anything, I took the Chinese medicine for the Chinese cold and guess what, *IT WORKED!*

This was my first weekend in China that I was awake during the day and had a normal sleeping schedule. My cold got better quickly, so I was shown around campus and I took some pictures. I can't say that I felt "at home" or "comfortable" in China, but I was adjusting to my new and different life.

That week-end I also did a lot of studying about China:

*   *   *   *

June's Brief History of China—Part II

The history of China during the 1900's is increasingly interesting and volatile. China was so weakened by civil unrest and the inability of the Qing Dynasty to reform ancient institutions that rebellions to overthrow the Qing's were inevitable. The Empress Dowager died in 1908 and the 2-year-old Emperor Puyi ascended to the throne obviously leaving the country with no real or image of leadership.

Sun Yatsen led an erratic uprising with disaffected Chinese troops. Three important principles which Sun established were Nationalism, Authority for the People and Livelihood for the People. Nationalism meant a national identity for the Chinese people with freedom from oppression by foreign powers including both the Manchus and the more recent European powers. Authority for the People meant a republican democracy with a constitution based on that of the United States, but it was doubtful to many realists that this would work in China because of the past extreme selfishness of men in power and the severe apathy among the peasants. Livelihood for the People included major economic reform of both agriculture and industry specifically excluding theories of Marx, which Sun Yatsen considered irrelevant to the problems of China. Sun also favored emancipation for women and ending the torturous foot binding.

The uprising he led could be called somewhat successful and a Provisional Republican Government was set up in late 1911 with representatives from seventeen provinces gathered in Nanjing and electing Sun Yatsen as the first temporary president.

The new government was not strong enough to force a Manchu abdication and so Yuan Shikai, head of the imperial army was called upon for assistance and support. Instead of helping, Yuan dissolved the new government, filled all political positions with his friends and supporters and made himself "president for life." Because of Yuan's long history of military power, Sun and his colleagues had no choice but to accept the terms Yuan offered. It had long been Yuan's dream to destroy the Manchu dynasty and replace it with his own. The problem was that he had few ideas to reform China. He had no ambitions beside his own power and glory. After time his imperial pretensions became a joke among the people. In humiliation and disappointment after less than 4 years, Yuan died and what followed was a period of warlords, none of whom were strong enough to nor wanted to bring the country together. Sun Yatsen, until he died from cancer in 1925, continued to try to set up a republican government in the South.

During this very chaotic time two very important political powers grew stronger, but the serious fighting with each other continually weakened them and the country. The Kuomintang or Nationalist Party finally established a government in 1928, which was lead by Chiang Kaishek who had, at times, worked as a personal agent of Sun Yatsen. Chiang, at the time was the only leader who knew what he wanted for China and was willing to do what he needed to do to gain popularity and success. He married the youngest sister of Madame Sun Yatsen and he was baptized in the Christian Methodist Church. The years from the late 1920's to the early 1930's were a period of prosperity and hope for some. Although for the vast majority of the people the constant problem was feeding themselves and no farming family could feel secure from one year to the next due to the numerous natural disasters that happened during this time including earthquakes, major flooding and famine. Chiang, emphasizing his Christian principles and admiration of the United States government for appearing to copy it, obtained general support in America, which increased and became most valuable with time. It is the basis of our currant protection of Taiwan.

It was one of the greatest weaknesses of the Nationalist Party that it was unable to produce policies and inspiration to obtain support for its programs. This is something that the Communists made use of. The Communist forces by 1930 had become an army of 40,000, but they had too many weak leaders. By 1934 the army had increased to one hundred thousand, but they were experiencing a grave defeat against Nationalist forces in south central China. Mao Zedong created unbelievable inspiration and legendary status during his Long March from 1934 to 1935. It began with a series of disasters and ended with a grim struggle against odds, with feats of heroism, hardship and ultimate survival. Great raging rivers were crossed as well as mountain peaks covered with snow and marshes of treacherous quicksand. Peace was achieved with non-Chinese tribes and respect was gained from all people by the honest dealings and ready payment for goods with silver dollars. Mao composed one of his most famous poems which the people loved. The Long March has been acclaimed as a triumph for Communism even though or maybe because, less than a tenth of the people reached the northwest. But greatest help of all for Communism was Japan and their various take-over attempts.

Chapter Nine:

My Great Teaching Idea

During my third week in China I started teaching the regular university classes. On three afternoons, I taught Advanced Spoken English classes to Juniors and Seniors. The classes met only once per week for 1½ hours, which really is not enough for improving speaking, but I would do my best to inspire them to want to improve.

I also had three university classes in the morning that I "co-taught" with Chinese teachers. It became obvious to me that the teachers were very weak in Spoken English. They held their English Department meetings in Chinese because no one wanted to take the risk of making an error in English, but they all really needed the practice. When I tried to speak and socialize with them, I received brief and muffled answers prefaced by a shy "my English is so poor." How could the students learn from teachers who could not speak freely themselves? I began to realize how important it was for me to be there, teaching Spoken English. I suggested the idea of co-teaching, which meant that the Chinese Teacher and I would be in the class together. I would teach part of the class and she would be there to listen (and hopefully learn herself) and then she would teach her part of the class giving the instruction and directions in Chinese and giving the homework. I really wanted to teach the English teachers, but I was told that they would be insulted because they really know English so well, but they were just very shy.

Then on Tuesday and Thursday nights I continued teaching the university teachers. During my 4th week I added a class on Monday and Wednesday nights which I called the Local Professionals. This class was advertised in the local newspaper and was open probably to anyone, who was willing to pay the tuition, but the people were supposed to have professional jobs and have a strong background in English and most of the students fit both criteria. Again, I was grateful to have more of a peer group to teach, but mostly I hoped to learn.

I also added one day, Tuesday, of traveling to a high school where I taught three English classes and had a wonderful banquet style lunch with their English teachers who were not too shy to talk with me.

I later found out that the real purpose of the Local Professionals' class and my going to the high school was to raise money to cover my salary and expenses. It cost the English Department a lot to have a foreign teacher because I was paid a little better than the Chinese teachers were because I taught extra classes and I needed to have decent housing, air-conditioning, a June-warmer (clothes dryer), airport pick-up service from the University driver and lots of other expenses. So, they had put me to work to "earn my own keep," but I really did not mind, although now looking back, it does make me feel used because they were not open with me about what they were doing. I found out that the university received the lion's share of what I earned and they gave me VERY little extra pay for all the extra work that I did. But, after all, I was the "kind and generous" American. I wish that I could have heard the other adjectives they used. That might have been a real "education" for me in China.

I much later found out that the high school paid my University twice as much as they paid me for "my use." I guess that it made me a little happy thinking that I "belonged" to the university in such a way that they could make so much money from my work.

My honest feelings were that I was in China to teach AND to learn, and the more experiences I had, the more I would benefit them and myself. I had one morning each week with no classes and nothing special to do. I seldom slept late, but this was my time to sometimes just lie in bed if I needed to until I was ready to get up. I needed just a little time to relax because I did not feel much pressure being in China. There was a definite cultural difference to deal with, but I was quickly learning the wonderful concept of detachment. I had no future in China beyond a year. I was a visitor and could feel amazingly detached whenever I wanted to. I guess that is the Buddhist idea that we are all visitors to earth in this life, and can be detached. I came to China to learn and just so I had enough free time to maintain my psychological well-being, I was much happier being busy.

I also gave some all-school lectures on Thursday afternoons. This was a time set aside for all departments to meet, so there were no classes. Since the English Department held their meetings in Chinese, there was little point in my being there. It was a good time to reach all the students who were not highly involved in sports. I had great attendance at my lectures.

I was very happy with my teaching schedule. I had lots of variety, but I could use similar lessons, slightly modified for each group so the preparation time was not too great. I loved having the adult classes where I hoped we could have more open discussions about their lives in China. I had to be somewhat careful about what I said and how I said it, but my thought was that these were adults and I could not be accused of damaging the minds of my students.

I also found another incredible way to learn more about my students. The head of the English department had told me that I was supposed to give written homework. That is hard to do in spoken English. At first I joked that they were to speak to the trees on a daily basis. This refers to the way the Chinese students had to get up every morning for their group exercises. Some mornings I could hear the loud speakers at a few minutes after 6 AM playing rousing loud music. The students were to jump out of bed, get dressed and go to their assigned spots, so attendance could be taken. They then had 15 to 20 minutes of exercises. After that they were to disburse on campus and spend about 45 minutes practicing English. There were spots all over campus for the students to sit and read out loud or to stand and "talk to the trees." Seriously many students used certain places on campus all day long, but I was not naïve enough to think that my students would really do this on a regular basis because I asked them to. The times of this overwhelming practice came when they had an eminent English test hanging over their heads. My class was a pleasure to most of my students, not such a threat.

But, I came up with a better idea. My reasoning was that spoken language written down could be called a letter. I asked my students to write me a weekly "love letter." I used the words "love letter" because I wanted them to approach it with urgency and passion. I said that I hoped they would really share their lives with me. Some of them, especially a few boys involved in sports gave me sparse and boring details of their weekly soccer games, not what I wanted, but maybe the best they could do. But, others poured out their little hearts telling me about their families and family problems, their loves and love problems, their studies and school problems, their future and career problems. I learned as much as I dreamed of learning about people. It turned out to be an absolutely brilliant idea. The letters were not a problem for me to read because often times I could hardly wait to get back to my apartment to read what they would tell me next. I could lie in my bed, under my warm blanket and receive the out-pouring of their hearts. I always made a brief comment after each letter. Sometimes I wrote a longer comment and each week I would select the most interesting and sometimes pressing letters and ask the student to have a private lunch or dinner with me. They considered that a real honor.

I made this assignment in all of my classes, but I knew that the Local Professionals and the University Teachers were too busy to write to me except perhaps occasionally about an important issue. But to my surprise one student started sending me letters that would haunt me for the rest of my life and change my life more than I ever dreamed possible.

Part II will show you many of his letters and tell you about how our friendship and trust developed.

PART TWO:

ROBERT'S EARLY LIFE IN CHINA

Editorial Comment:

This part contains letters written to me by Robert in the University Teachers' class. I need to explain that I made as few corrections as possible to his letters. I thought that his English was reasonably good and understandable. Sometimes he had unusual word usage or sentence construction that I wanted to leave as he had written it to make it his own expression. Sometimes, being a teacher, there were things that I felt I had to correct. He did give me permission to make any changes I felt necessary, but I tried to limit them as much as possible to only what I thought was needed for clearer understanding.

CHAPTER ONE:

AN EXCEPTIONAL BEGINNING

To my great surprise, after I presented the assignment I was giving all of my classes, I started receiving letters from the older man in my University Teachers' class. He was a retired teacher and obviously had more time than the others did. But, soon I was to find out that he also had, more importantly, an amazing story to tell about his life in China that I would later be compelled to tell others, like you.

Letter # 1 from your student, Robert

Dear American Teacher,

I was born in 1929 to a merchant family in Hangzhou. At the time of my birth, I already had three sisters and two brothers.

My grandfather was one of the wealthy and important businessmen in Hangzhou having set up a silk and satin factory and a workshop for manufacturing fans. These are some of the famous products of Hangzhou.

My grandfather had many sons and daughters, but he lived with us. Our residence was so big in the traditional Chinese style having three halls and three courtyards with a small garden.

Owing to the riches of my grandfather, his sons and daughters did not have to work.

My parents liked this because they could sleep until the sun was three poles high. Many days I came home from classes at noon and they were still sleeping. In the afternoon they played mahjong pieces and watched dramas at night. They had a life of unbelievable leisure and comfort.

There were about ten servants and each child was under the care of a wet nurse. I was the first child, for some reason, suckled by my mother herself so she made a special pet of me.

I can remember that my grandfather sat on the sofa in his study all day as a serious and dignified man. These are the impressions of my early childhood before the War of Resistance against Japan (1937–1945) which in the West is called World War II.

Dear Teacher, I hope that this interests you and that you are happy to receive my letter.

Sincerely, Robert

I was very happy to receive this letter and it was interesting to me that Robert was from Hangzhou. I had been offered a teaching position at a university in Hangzhou, but I knew very little about China. I later found out that Hangzhou is a very beautiful city and that anyone who knows anything about China would have taken that job simply for the location.

I had not as yet done any traveling around China, but after reading Robert's letters, I put it in my plans to visit Hangzhou during the summer. After spending only a short while in Hangzhou, I realized that it was one of the most beautiful cities in China and in many ways became one of my favorites. It is one of the famous popular tourist destinations. One reason is that West Lake, which the city was built beside, is a large freshwater lake bordered on three sides by hills. The banks and islands are blanketed with gardens and temples. There is an old Chinese saying that, "In heaven there is paradise, on earth Suzhou and Hangzhou."

It was very impressive to know that Robert had been born into such wealth. I have seen several large houses as he said he had lived in that are now set up as museums. The Chinese style of houses is quite different from our homes in the West. Each "hall" as it is called, is like a large formal living room with special seating for each family member according to rank and position. People also often took their meals in the room, brought in by servants. The kitchen was quite far removed from the living area and was basically outdoors except for a roof and some partial walls.

There were many side rooms adjacent to each hall for sitting, as sleeping rooms or for storage of personal items. The courtyards are huge enclosed outdoor areas for living when the weather is favorable. In the past, women were often confined to their homes and did not go out for shopping, which was done by servants. These courtyards provided a way for women to get fresh air and sunshine without having to leave home. There might be chairs for sitting, couches for reclining and tables for eating. There can be trees, plants and flowers placed all over the outdoor room. I imagine the little garden had a pond with fish and a stream with possibly a small open-air building for creating shade. I'm sure that there were large rocks and beautiful plants tended by at least one gardener and possibly more.

The number of servants was great, but they not only waited on their assigned family member, but also may have helped prepare food, which in China, is a huge project. Another less pleasant task the servants had was to bring in little portable toilets when needed. They waited on the families every need. Servants and even slaves were very common in the history of China. Girl babies were of little value to peasants who had to work the fields, joined by their sons as soon as they were old enough. A mother might keep one daughter to help her, but after that, female babies were often sold as slaves or servants as soon as they were old enough to take care of themselves and work, which was young, maybe four, five or six.

I can't wait to tell Robert how much this interests me. I hoped he would have another letter after our next class and this is what I was given:

Letter #2 from your student, Robert

Dear American Teacher,

After the wonderful beginning to my life, I want to tell you what happened next.

After July 7, 1937, when Japan invaded China our way of life was changed, unbelievably.

In the autumn of 1937, one confusing night, by kerosene light, many servants tied much baggage and many possessions to a cart. It was all carried away. An old servant led my family riding in several rickshaws (2 wheeled vehicles pulled by men). We got to the side of the river and had a long wait. We could see the Changjiang Bridge had been badly damaged by explosives. This very high bridge had two levels, the upper was a highway for vehicles and the lower was a railway. It had been blown up to obstruct the Japanese from going forward. There were huge crowds of people under either end of the bridge, but I do not know why they were there.

In the stillness of midnight a little boat came quietly. We embarked, eleven people total, including my family, an old maidservant and a fifteen year-old slave girl. All our baggage filled almost half of the boat. I got into a corner and sat on a leather suitcase.

The night was very out of the ordinary with its dead silence. Our boat swayed gently in the water and as it moved forward with a creak, soon I fell asleep. Being only eight I could not manage to stay awake even with my heart pounding and my head swimming in as much confusion as the river.

The next day the boat sailed into a little river where there were shops along the bank. A basket filled with "aous", a native product of dried bean curd, was tied to a pole and stretched out to our boat. We attached money to the basket in return.

I felt so strange wondering what really was happening. My first years had been so filled with peace and security, but those days were over. I had no idea what lied ahead in my life. Dear Teacher, can you imagine the fear that I felt, the confusion and the dread for my future?

Sincerely, Robert

This was quite a period to be living through. I was very curious to find out what happened next and if all of Robert's family survived the Japanese occupation which I had heard was brutal.

Chapter Two:

The Japanese Kill Many Chinese

Letter # 3 from your student, Robert

Dear American Teacher,

The next dark midnight a loud sound awoke me. We had found the family of the man who managed our factory in Hangzhou. They received us in Shaoxing, which was a rural area outside the big city and the man's native home. It was a beautiful village with many canals and rivers. I now know that it was likened to Venice.

We left the boat and a man with a lantern led us into the residence. According to communist class analysis, it maybe was considered a land-lord class home.

I finally found out why we had left our home in Hangzhou. Word of the Nangjing Massacre had reached the people of Hangzhou and many decided to flee their homes in fear of their lives. I did not understand at the time what a horrible thing this was.

We began a new style of living so different from in Hangzhou. There was no electricity so we used kerosene lamps. My family moved into a fairly new, but already established house in the rear of the main house.

For a boy, not knowing the fear and gravity of our life style change and the horrors that were taking place in China, we lived a happy life in the new place. In the village there was a river in front of the square and land for growing field crops in the rear. In the distance, mountains could be dimly seen in the morning mist. It was as beautiful as a picture.

There were many happy childhood activities like swimming, paddling, picking shells, racing and flying kites with many children playing together. It was a wonder being a child and of being able to always find joy and distractions. I had no idea of the grief and desolation felt by the adults because their world of luxury and idleness had passed. It was years before I would know that the terror and hopelessness of thinking of the future was even worse than the sadness and depression when thinking of the past.

The village made a lasting impression on me with the people being diligent, thrifty and living in harmony. I lived in Shaoxing Village for three years and it gave me many happy childhood memories. The three years seemed like a very long time to a child.

Our first year in Shaoxing my tenth brother was born. Hangzhou fell to the Japanese and we lost our factory and everything we owned.

Sincerely, Robert

I suddenly realized that I had better study more about the history of China.

*   *   *   *

June's Brief History of China—Part III

The Japanese took advantage of the fighting between the Kuomintang and the Communists and the confusion it created. They invaded Manchuria where they set up a puppet state with the last Chinese emperor, Puyi, as its symbolic head.

Finally in 1936, a shaky anti-Japanese alliance was formed between the Communists and Kuomintang, but it did little to stop the advance of the Japanese whom in 1937, launched and all-out invasion of China. By 1939, they had overrun most of eastern China and in 1941; Japan brazenly expanded its aggression by attacking the United States at Pearl Harbor which ultimately and thankfully brought its downfall.

The Kuomintang-Communist alliance collapsed in 1941, when open resistance to Japan became futile. Strangely enough while Japan occupied China, the Civil War between these two groups continued to take place. But, fighting Japan had to become the first priority. The brunt of fighting the Japanese was borne by the Nationalists and within eighteen months the Nationalists were driven from Nanjing to Chongqing.

The policy of Japan toward China has been described as one of deliberate intimidation coupled with total ruthlessness and indifference to the people. The most famous evidence of this was the Nanjing Massacre in 1937. I have been to the Memorial to the Nanjing Massacre. There are exhibits that document the atrocities committed by the Japanese soldiers against the civilian population during the occupation of Nanjing. As many as three hundred thousand civilian people may have died. There are pictures of actual executions taken by Japanese army photographers. What is most shocking is not only what happened, but that the Japanese took such graphic photographs of the events. The most difficult sight is a gruesome viewing hall built over a mass grave of massacre victims.

Also, while in Nanjing, I visited the immense Sun Yatsen Mausoleum which was begun a year after his death. He is considered by both the Communists and the Kuomintang to be the "Father of Modern China." His tomb is built as a Ming-style tomb with a stone gateway of Fujian marble, an enormous stone stairway and a crypt at the top of the steps at the rear of the memorial Chamber. A prostrate marble statue of Dr. Sun seals his coffin. It is a very impressive place that is absolutely magnificent and Chinese are allowed to visit it with great reverence.

Japan's time in China is one of many horror stories including terrible things the Chinese did in desperation to fight them. An example is the breaking of the Yellow River dikes to halt the Japanese advance into Henan in 1938. The floods engulfed homes, towns and farmlands. Communist criticism was strong regarding this enormous disregard for life and this flooding must rank as one of the greatest man-made misfortunes of history.

Once the U.S. declared war on Japan, the U.S. became the total focus of Japan's fighting energy. The Japanese position in China remained static because they had already gained all that they had wanted from China and were now fighting for survival.

At one time there was an Allied plan that an invasion of Japan would be launched from Shandong after a reconquest of the peninsula. But the dropping of the two atomic bombs on the Japanese cities of Hiroshima and Nagasaki ended the war suddenly and decisively when Japan agreed to an unconditional surrender. Japanese troops were withdrawn from China.

*　　　*　　　*　　　*

I also had to carefully check a map of China because I had never heard of Shaoxing. It is just 67 km south-east of Hangzhou and is the center of a waterway system. People who have been to Venice consider those who praise Shaoxing as "China's Venice" to be a great exaggeration because it is not as large. But the area is notable for its rivers and would be a good place to live as a child. It also has been an important agricultural market.

Is it not wonderful to be a child and be able to live obliviously to all the heartbreak and horrors surrounding you? Robert gratefully did have a few happy years in his childhood.

I was really looking forward to his next letters.

I received letters from my college students also. Many times, immediately after class I would jump into my soon-to-be warm bed and lay under the covers for hours reading their letters. I did not know what a brilliant idea this was to learn about life in China. None of my students had stories of such an epic nature as Robert's, but family life in China was none the less very interesting to learn about.

Letter #4 from your student, Robert

Dear American Teacher,

To seek a livelihood and for studying, my father, older sisters and older brother went to Shanghai. My mother, two sisters, three brothers, the slave girl and I still stayed in the village. We studied in the town's primary school, a regular school of considerable extent. In this school we began to accept the idea of resistance against Japan.

There were many mosquitoes in the village. I suffered from malaria. The whole village contracted dysentery. While I recovered, my second brother (sixteen years old) and my younger brother (two years old) became ill at the same time. In the village we could not see a doctor. In only nine days my little brother died. My second brother got amebic dysentery and died after six months. This is the first time I experienced real loss and suffering in my childish heart. Now the Japanese owed us a blood debt because we learned that they had sprinkled the bacillus in the river.

During the three years in Shaoxing Village I had only studied one year and my sister had studied to grade six in two years.

Then in 1940 we returned to Hangzhou. Our beautiful old home was already a scene of desolation. My family was poor. At the time my father got a job at a textile mill and my oldest sister became a teacher in a primary school. I studied until I was old enough to go to Shanghai to a junior middle school.

But, then things got worse. In the summer of 1942 my father died of typhoid fever. We had to sell the big house in Hangzhou for money needed to survive.

Sincerely, Robert

Chapter Three:

From the Japanese to the Kuomintang

Letter #5 from your student, Robert

Dear American Teacher,

In 1943 I returned to Hangzhou from school in Shanghai.

Until this time I had just seen Japanese soldiers. They were not a terrible image. They were highly disciplined and never infringed on common people.

Of course, the people of Nanjing felt differently after the massacre, but Hangzhou lived a calm life and nothing so terrible happened in our city.

In 1945, one night, suddenly a large group of soldiers playing The Double Eagle March came onto the street. Jubilant crowds surged towards them. The troops were divided in two with Chinese troops on the left and American troops on the right. They marched from west to east. People warmly applauded them. The war of resistance against aggression was over. Japan was defeated in China.

These eight years of my life seemed like they were actually half a century long. It was the Japanese who injured us—all of China had been damaged and especially my family and my home. Then the Japanese were driven away. I think I will always be grateful to Americans.

Sincerely, Robert

It became obvious to me after several months of living in China that still to this day the Chinese hate the Japanese and I believe they always will. Numerous times students made negative comments about the Japanese. Whenever I felt it was acceptable I would say, "What can really be said against the Japanese? They have done nothing worse than what the Chinese themselves have done to their own people." I was speaking historically about all the fighting that had taken place in China with various kingdoms and warlords. I was not thinking of what I learned and you will soon read about that had happened to Robert.

Letter #6 from your student, Robert

Dear American Teacher,

The Kuomintang came to take over. They were being supported by the American government. I heard it was because they prayed to the same god. Their headquarters were in Chongqing. They wantonly plundered and took people's property. The biggest embezzler and head of military police named Mei was finally executed to calm the people's anger.

From 1945 to 1949 the Koumintang recovered and ruled. In these four years the various troops disturbed people so often that they got to the point of not being able to tolerate it any longer. Soldiers and disabled soldiers traveled or resided in public places. In the theater, they would enter with no admission ticket. They would ride a rickshaw without paying. One day a government officer rode a rickshaw and stopped before our school. He didn't pay the fare, but instead hit the coulee. This aroused the indignation of many of my schoolmates. We over-powered the man, took his gun and handed him to our school military instructor. But, he was quickly released and we feared retaliation for weeks.

People bitterly hated the Koumintang for its corruption and cruelty to the common man.

The Communist party launched a war against Koumintang. Prices skyrocketed and people could not support themselves. People broke into a rice store and others tried to seize a bank. Public order was in a state of chaos.

The Communist party enjoyed the ardent support of the people, especially the students. We all thought the Communist Party could save China. It was confusing when students held the first demonstration against the Chinese Communist Party and USSR because they had betrayed Mongolia.

I studied at the senior middle school grade three and my brother was at University. Shanghai students protested the Chinese Communist party betraying Outer Mongolia to USSR and held demonstrations. Before this all demonstrations had been against the Koumintang. There was a famous slogan:

we want democracy,
we want freedom,
we want food.

Sincerely, Robert

It was time for more Chinese History:

＊   ＊   ＊   ＊

June's Brief History of China—Part IV

Bloodshed continued in China as an all-out civil war fighting for control of the country was waged. At the beginning of open conflict the Communist Forces numbered a little more than one million, and the soldiers of the Nationalists were three times as many. Though Nationalist troops held the cities and railway lines, almost all the countryside was dominated by the Communists. The United States was backing the Nationalists and the Soviet Union understandably supported the Communist Forces.

A dramatic power struggle began as the Kuomintang and Communist forces gathered in Manchuria for the final showdown. By 1948, the Communists had captured so much U.S.-supplied Kuomintang equipment and had recruited so many Kuomintang soldiers that they equaled the Kuomintang in both numbers and supplies. Three great battles were fought in 1948 and 1949 in which the

Kuomintang were defeated and hundreds of thousands of Kuomintang troops joined the Communists. The Communists moved south and crossed the Yangzi and by October all the major cities in southern China had fallen to them.

In Beijing on October 1, 1949, Mao Zedong proclaimed the foundation of the People's Republic of China. Chiang Kaishek fled to the island of Formosa taking with him the entire gold reserves of the country and what was left of the air force and the navy. In addition, two million soldiers and refugees fled from the mainland. The United States, which had been backing Chiang Kaishek, protected his move and prevented further attack. President Truman ordered a protective naval blockade.

Another political situation that Robert mentions is what he calls the betrayal of Outer Mongolia. The New Chinese Communist Government had many disputes along the border with the Soviet Union. The two governments easily agreed that Xinjiang would remain Chinese. Other areas were not so easy to settle because the Chinese felt that in the past Russian imperialism and aggression had forced agreements on their predecessors.

Mongolia had been a long disputed region with its border literally drawn in the sand of the Gobi Desert. And it had long been divided with the Russian Empire setting up a "protectorate" over the northern part of Mongolia. The Chinese governed the rest of Mongolia until 1911, with the fall of the Qing's, when it became an independent state. For a while it had the name, The Mongolian People's Republic, but during the War between China and Japan, parts of it too were occupied by the Japanese. In 1936, Mao Zedong said that when the people's revolution has been victorious in China, the Outer Mongolian Republic would automatically become part of the Chinese federation, at its own will. But, in fact, in February 1950, a treaty was signed settling the independence of Outer Mongolia and few Chinese people have accepted the loss of this territory.

Chapter Four:

A Successful Graduation from University

Letter # 7 from your student, Robert

Dear American Teacher,

In 1948 & 1949 I studied at a famous university in Shanghai. Launched from the student union, students held demonstrations all over the city. Mayor Wu Guo Zhen (a famous man in China) came to mediate. He was pushed and shoved by the students and his spectacles and pipe fell to the ground.

* * *

A flying tank (a black arresting vehicle) was sent out to suppress students. Several students were wounded and arrested. Some Communist student leaders leading the demonstrations were arrested, but after two weeks they were set free.

This is how the Koumintang would be defeated. They at last met defeat when in May 1949, the Communist Party entered and was stationed in Shanghai. They did not commit the slightest offense against the civilians. They even slept in the streets. We asked them to rest in rooms that were empty. They would not do it. (This was only during the initial stages of power that they behaved so perfectly.) They were strict in discipline. There was presented a striking contrast between the Communist party and the Koumintang. In society and in camps the Communists were full of vigor and vitality.

You can see how after first suffering under the cruel Japanese and then the corruption of the Kuomintang, we finally held out hope for the wonderful Communist party.

Dear Teacher, can you understand having such hopes for Communism after what we had experienced with the Japanese and Koumintang?

Sincerely, Robert

Letter #8 from your student, Robert

Dear American Teacher,

After six months the university made known the list of the Communist Party members and a new democratic Youth League of China was set up. Later it would become the Communist Youth League.

I joined the Youth League and we often held meetings until midnight, which interfered greatly with my studies. When we were not meeting I was so busy studying. It was my natural disposition now to work very hard. I had strong discipline as a student. I was not a good League member from the start to the finish. Gradually I found the party occupied too commanding of a position in my life, conflicting so much with my studies.

I felt that the League looked down on the masses and our important goals to improve our lives through education. The League was supposed to mean everything to us and be more important than anything else in our lives. That to me seemed foolish and not truly productive for ourselves or the country. How could we more greatly improve ourselves and our country than studying hard to receive the best possible education?

Many students were against the League Organization. A meeting was held to inquire the way to deal with this situation. I deeply felt there was great antagonism between the party and the masses. Many negative things were said out loud. Afterwards these upper level schoolmates graduated and got jobs, but in 1955, in the movement for the elimination of counterrevolutionaries they were pronounced guilty and put in prison, for many years.

There were three political movements being launched from 1950 to 1952. In 1950, the movement to suppress counter-revolution was fierce, but lasted for a short time. Only a few students were arrested.

From 1951 to 1952 there was a movement against The Three Evils of corruption, waste and bureaucracy within the Party, government, army and mass organization.

There also was a movement Against Five Evils of bribery, tax evasion, theft of state property, cheating on government contracts and stealing of economic information. In the early stage it was directed at activities as practiced by owners of private industrial and commercial enterprises. In the later stage this was directed against business circles, and in the end, in order to magnify the problem, the evils were applied to the masses.

Therefore, at that time many many men took their own lives rather than face the severe harassment, persecution and who knew what other consequences. Saving face was still a strong concept in Chinese society. There were two acquaintances in my university who died in such a way. In the end, many matters were left unsettled. But, it was too late for those who had already settled matters themselves.

Before I graduated in the summer of 1952, the Communist party launched a movement called Ideological Remolding. This movement was aimed at students and the goal was that schoolmates must confess their political ideals and other ideals. If they were not confessed in a satisfactory way, the student would not graduate. Therefore in 1952, my last term at the university, we almost couldn't study the subjects of our degree. We held meetings all day until midnight working on writing out our ideals so the Communist Party would allow us to graduate. But, at last, all the students were passed and I received my degree.

Sincerely, Robert

Chapter Five:

The Hope of
Communism Dies

I needed to learn more about the early days of the Chinese Communist Party.

✳   ✳   ✳   ✳

June's Brief History of China—Part V

In its early years the Communist government was remarkably successful in establishing its power and restoring a measure of well being and prosperity to the people of China. Land reform brought some equality to the countryside. The Marriage Law offered some rights to women, although it did weaken the position of the individual. Of course, the ending of Civil War brought an immediate improvement in the economy and a new national sense of pride and accomplishment. Also, there was the psychological improvement that comes from relieving the constant fears of danger and death from both war and internal fighting.

Throughout the country propaganda and what was called "persuasion" were used to ensure acceptance of the new regime. People who had never shown any interest in politics were required to join demonstrations. This gave people a sense of participation in government that they had never had. It was also very effective in binding them to the causes they now publicly endorsed. In kindergartens and schools, even in the poorest communities, children were taught slogans and songs supporting the government and the party. They were urged to tell their parents and elders of the new morality and to criticize or report those who failed to live up to it. In all circumstances, the Communists taught the people, each individual should consider the good of the whole, and no single person was entitled to excess advantage or privilege. Most importantly the new Communist administrators were honest and courteous in their behavior toward the people. The actions and attitude of strong party members was impeccable and this goal continues to today in many party members who I talked with on campus. Party members consider themselves to be better than other people and we all know what that can lead to.

Of course, not everything was wonderful for everyone. In many regions of China, the redistribution of land gave opportunity for mass meetings, which often instituted violence against wealthy men and their families. Many of these landlords and rich peasants decided to purge their wrong doings before assemblies of local citizens. Often they were then permitted to take a place (a much lower one than before) in the new communist society. Emotions ran high and atrocities were reported where men were shot or hanged by vindictive mobs. The death toll is not known, but for sure several hundred thousand people were accused, condemned and murdered in legalized lynch courts.

Under the new Communist regime, slogans and campaigns attacked private individual relationships and people were urged to direct all their energies to national service under the leadership of the party. The Marriage Law of 1950, although giving needed rights to women also provided opportunity for direct involvement of the Communist Party in the daily private lives of the people.

Women were often forced to criticize their husbands in public political meetings and children were taught in school to denounce their parents. Often elderly women enjoyed a new power and became the most energetic informants and enforcers of local Communist control. The town gossips now had unbelievable power.

In 1953, it was announced that the traditional peasant life, with each family being responsible for the produce of its own fields, would be changed to a system of rural co-operatives and communes, with all land held by the community and all labor given to common service. Immediately, there were disagreements over the division of labor between energetic and competent farmers and those that were lazy and inefficient. There were many problems and great resistance in some places to this new system, which had greater advantages for the Communist government than for the people involved. On strictly economic grounds, the pooling of resources gave more opportunity for the purchase of modern machinery, which was too expensive for any individual. A second advantage for the Party was control and prevention of private wealth and personal profit. There was also direct control of every aspect of farming and their personal lives in communes where there was no family privacy. There were quotas of production and the collection of revenue for the government was easier than it had ever been before.

Besides the drastic changes in agriculture the other area of development was industrial production to provide a domestic supply of machinery and chemicals. Considered a major achievement was the reconstruction of the Anshan Iron and Steel Works in Manchuria south of Shenyang where Robert went after graduation.

During the First Five-Year Plan from 1953 to 1957, the economy of China most likely achieved a growth rate of six percent. This new prosperity was shared throughout the whole country, but it was obtained at the cost of considerable cruelty to many who were regarded as "enemies" of the people simply because they were better educated or had been born into a more fortunate past.

Letter #9 from your student, Robert

Dear American Teacher,

In 1952, after graduation I was assigned to the Anshan Integrated Iron and Steel Works in what is now the province of Liaoning in northeastern China, not very far from Dalian. In that year it was also the beginning of the first Five-Year Plan of the Communist Government.

One train, filled with over one thousand graduates from Shanghai made the journey to their new work together. We gathered, in force, at the Anshan Iron and Steel Company. We were told that all the country was in support of us because iron and steel were so important to China's future. In that time, we felt deeply stable, arrogant and ready to give our lives for the motherland.

In 1952 to 1953 another movement was launched this one with the goal to "maintain secrecy." This was a small-scale movement, but it created much grief and heartache for so many people. I have a cousin who had a job in Shenyang and her boyfriend was working in Harbin. Shenyang and Harbin are both in northeastern China with Harbin being farther northeast. If you want to go from Harbin to Shanghai you must pass Shenyang. That year they agreed to meet at Shenyang and go to Shanghai for their marriage ceremony. On the appointed day my cousin waited for his train to arrive at the railway station, but he never came. My cousin did not know what to do. She was so disappointed and feared that perhaps he had changed his mind and did not want her. People tried to contact him but he could not be reached and no one at his work had seen or heard from him. For a very long time there was not a single word about him or any message from him. At last there was a rumor that he had been arrested at the station because he had taken a drawing back to his apartment to work on in the evening. He was not heard from for three years.

Since my cousin did not know what really happened she tried to go on with her life. In 1955 just as she was going to be married to another man, her first boyfriend was released and he, at last, made the trip to Shenyang. After much personal grief for many people and careful consideration, my cousin decided to marry the first boyfriend.

Sincerely, Robert

Letter #10 from your student, Robert

Dear American Teacher,

In 1955 there was another movement, this one for the elimination of counter-revolutionaries. This time the movement was popularized for the whole people. One location for counter-revolutionary action was at Hutfeng and it became known as the Hutfeng Counter-revolutionary Group.

The Hutfeng Counter-revolutionary Group picked up my uncle (the husband of my mother's sister). My uncle had been interrogated and criticized all day and into the night. For some reason, after he was released in the middle of the night, he lay on the road and was run over and killed. Many thought that he actually took his own life. He left behind his wife and five children. There were no jobs available for such widowed women and their lives and those of their children would be hard to imagine. No one could provide relief for my aunt and no one dared to help her. A large number of people were arrested and/or murdered in strange ways in this movement.

A colleague of mine was arrested, with the accusation for something he did during the period of the War of Resistance against Japan. He had been an interpreter for the US Army at Yannan—on the Burma Highway. He had also been the head of the Koumintang's broadcasting station. So he was considered now to be a counter-revolutionary. The evidence was that they searched his home and found a radio receiver. He was immediately cast into prison. After nine months he was set free on what was called an inculcated release. An inculcated release means that it was decided the person could not be held responsible because the misbehavior was from the past. It was decided that some people should not have to pay retroactive punishment. This colleague of mine was older and had graduated eight years ago from Shanghaii Communications University. He had an old mother, a wife and six children who were not supported during his imprisonment. During that time his mother got a mental disease due to her anxiety and concern for their lives.

Several close schoolmates and I subsidized his family five yuan/month in secret. At that time our wages were fifty yuan every month. It was a dangerous thing for us to do, but we admired him and had great esteem for him. He was very intelligent and a great thinker.

From 1953 to 1955 he had lead four workers, I was one of them, to translate "Automatic Control of Rolling Mill." (Russian edition) We had learned Russian at Anshan Iron and Steel Co. When we gathered at his home for translating the book, there were many spies arranging around. He was looked at with suspicion and he also was proud and somewhat arrogant about his abilities with foreign languages. He looked down upon the leaders and that was the real reason for his arrest.

Sincerely, Robert

Letter #11 from your student, Robert

Dear American Teacher,

Generally speaking, young people placed their hopes on the Communist Party. I did too without exception, but after so many incidents. I could no longer feel hopeful or positive. I felt that they did not take the masses (the common people) into account. They had become imperious and despotic. They did not keep their word to the masses, no one had the right to say anything against them, and they bullied and oppressed anyone they wanted.

In 1954 a civil war in Vietnam had just finished. Vietnam had just been divided into two parts. Part of the truce agreement stipulated that neither of the two Vietnams was permitted to station foreign troops. In very little time Northern Vietnam began a civil war. Yun You Sou was the deputy to the Northern Vietnam Communist Party and he also launched a civil war in the Southern Vietnam. China had secretly joined in the fighting in both places. At that time, I saw through the Communist Party's swindle to the people. I started to look upon the Communist Party as my enemy.

In 1956 the situation in the country seemed to be getting better, but then there was a new movement of reform for privately owned industrial and commercial enterprises. There was still some capitalism in this area of the economy. But, private enterprises in the whole country were reformed as joint state-private enterprises in one night. Some brave people beat drums and gongs in the streets to protest. I wonder what happened to them, but I shutter to think of it.

Sincerely, Robert

CHAPTER SIX:

A HUNDRED FLOWERS
AND LOVE GET TRAMPLED

It was time to study more Chinese history:

*   *   *   *

June's Brief History of China—Part VI

In 1956 Chairman Mao Zedong made a speech urging that among artists and writers 'a hundred flowers should blossom,' and among men of science 'let all the schools of thought contend.' Despite this open encouragement for criticism and debate, most intellectuals knew better and were cautious and did not respond. Late in 1956 it began to appear that the government was in fact considering a policy of relaxation. Gradually in 1957, university professors and students joined in expressing objections to the rigidity of the Party, inefficiency, arrogance and selfishness of Communist cadres.

It is certain that the rulers of China never expected the response they got and it appeared to them that things were getting out of hand. By June, limits were placed that commentary could no longer be made against the policies of socialism. By July, critics were under personal attack as rightist elements. They were harangued and humiliated in public until they confessed to their faults and errors in ideology.

For intellectuals, writers, thinkers, professors and students of the universities, the destruction of the Hundred Flowers marked the end of an era and the demise of a dream. The hopes that so many had for Communism were permanently destroyed.

Basically, no government like the Communist regime in China can tolerate open and vocal opposition. The enforcement of censorship is limited only by the government's power, which must remain limitless. A Chinese intellectual has been quoted as saying, "It has been said that tyranny makes men cynical; now we know that a republic, as the one in China, makes men silent." (Human Rights in China, 1989)

Letter # 12 from your student, Robert

Dear American Teacher,

I must tell you about the woman whom I wanted to marry. I mentioned her once in class when we talked about human rights. I said that I had wanted the right to love and marry. You didn't seem to understand what I meant, so I will tell you more. In autumn of 1954, my sister graduated from Shanghaii and was assigned to work in Shenyang at a pharmaceutical factory. It was two hours by railway from Anshan. In 1955 on New Year's, I went to see my sister.

There I met a school mate of my sister. She was 6 years younger than I. Afterwards, we saw each other again and again and began falling in love. In 1956 we were engaged in Shanghai. We suffered many problems in our love affair. First, we had no money and second, there was no time to be together. In April 1957, she was moved to the Shanghai Medical Institute because she had developed some kind of disease. She could both receive treatment and work there. To travel from Anshan to Shanghai would take a month of my wages to make a round trip and then there would be no money left to live on. Until 1962, I had only twenty days leave each year, including Sundays. We only made use of seven days off. The usual Chinese holidays are New Year's Day, May 1 (Labor Day), October 1st (National Day) and Spring Festival which is the Chinese New Year. The time together was precious to us as you can imagine.

In April of 1957, the Communist party in the whole country organized discussions, listening carefully to the views of the intellectuals. All intellectuals were asked for a—"free airing of views." Da zi bao or big character posters were to say all we thought without reserve. The party was told to not seize on someone's mistakes or shortcomings and do not come down with the big stick on anyone's ideas. I had been invited to make a speech on liberty and democracy. By Sept 15th there were many critical articles (Da Zi Bao) put up around my office.

My original plan was that I would go to Shanghai to get married on National Day—which was October 1, 1957. But, like soap bubbles, my marriage plans burst and vanished. It made both my fiancée and me heartbroken.

After criticism of me as a rightist, I was not allowed to attend my own work. I had to go to the library every day to prepare self-critical material. Every other day meetings were held to criticize me and expose my words and deeds that were in opposition to the Party. At the meetings they criticized me and I had to criticize myself. At that time, in 1957, criticism meetings were held with civility, and they did not resort to force. Possibly the reason is that they were dealing with educated intellectuals who were not as disposable as the masses.

In August of 1958, I was confirmed as a rightist of the second kind. Rightists are classified as six different kinds. The first and second kinds are considered heavy convicts and they are serious prisoners doing penal labor under surveillance with no wage. Strangely, for my punishment, I was to be given living expenses of twenty yuan/month which was then one fifth of my regular wages, and I was allowed to continue my very important work at Anshan Iron and Steel.

The Communist party had declared that the first or second kinds of rightists also could seek livelihood by themselves. In fact, I thought that was impossible, but I wanted nothing but to go to Shanghai to see my fiancée and get married. I made this request with no hope in my heart.

Sincerely, Robert

Letter #13 from your student, Robert

Dear American Teacher,

One day the propaganda department of Anshan Iron and Steel summoned me and admonished me to not think of leaving. They said that if I am not well behaved, they would cast me into prison—there was nothing strange about that. That was just what the Communist Party said and often times did to have control over people.

They knew that I was thinking of leaving because of my fiancée. I no longer received letters from her. She could not write to me again because her political organization asked her to make a clean break with me. She must cut off our relationship from now on, if not her father would write to me to beg me not to also jeopardize her future.

I realized how stupid I had been to trust anything the Communists said. I should have known better. I felt that I had caused all these problems myself, by being so naive.

I decided that I wanted to seek a livelihood by myself. I really wanted nothing but to see my fiancée and be married.

Sincerely, Robert

Chapter Seven:

Life Deteriorates Even More

Dear American Teacher,

The anti-rightist struggle was ended in 1958. I was transferred out of my regular work unit to do manual labor. It gave me many valuable experiences. I saw many Russian installations. I also narrated our translation of "Automatic Control of Rolling Mills" from Russian. I personally benefited considerably from this time.

I basically lived in solitude for those two years. My schoolmates were assigned to other locations around the country. The remaining acquaintances I had kept clear of me and dared not even talk to me. I worked from dawn to dusk and read famous literary works in the remaining time.

The only dream I had left was to become a fugitive of China and go abroad. I dreamed of secretly escaping on a foreign ship on the Huangpu River in Shanghai. My brother had graduated from an "ocean-shipping" college and I learned from him the patterns of how ships passed in and out of port. My plan was that I would hide in a cabin. The only problem was that if you were discovered or were betrayed by foreigners, your life

would be over unless you could swim hundreds of miles. And so, I only
dreamed it, there was no such chance and I really did not have the courage to try regardless how desperate I felt.

Sincerely, Robert

*   *   *   *

June's Brief History of China—Part VII

By the end of the First Five-Year Plan in 1957, the Communists had achieved
many real successes. The gross output value of agriculture doubled from 1949 to
1957. The output value of industry rose over five hundred per cent. Factory output almost trebled. Much of the improvement could be attributed to peacetime
recovery, but the Communist Government took all of the credit.

The concept of the Great Leap Forward was completely different from the
strategy of the First Five-Year Plan. There were reasons for a new approach.

In many respects the country remained backward with too great of a population of poor peasants. If the people of the countryside were mobilized there was a
chance the entire nation would improve.

At the center of the new strategy was a system of people's communes, which
was proclaimed as a vital unit of the economy. The communes brought official
authority and propaganda closer to each citizen. The Great Leap Forward was
presented by propaganda as the will of the people mobilized to overthrow any
negative. The problem is that there is a limit to what can be willed. There are two
good examples. On the North China Plain there was a vast program of well-drill-
ing to increase water for the crops. The problem was that the enthusiastic people
did not realize that the water was brackish and actually reduced the fertility of the
land. Another program was for 'backyard blast furnaces." But, it was discovered
that small-scale plants with erratic temperature and quality control could never
produce reliable pig iron and were totally useless for the production of steel. They
actually turned good ore into trash.

The Great Leap Forward, by the speed with which it expanded enterprise and
by its encouragement of local authority disrupted and taxed to the limit Communist administration. And with so much enthusiasm for great progress even greater

progress was reported. The problem was that it was not accurate. Both the planning and the boom in the economy got out of hand and information sent to Beijing was quite inaccurate. The greatest problem was poor administration. Unit leaders all vied with each other to announce higher levels of production. It took some time before planners recognized and admitted the deception that was being practiced.

Sometimes decisions were based on this inaccurate information such as switching vast areas of land from growing grain to growing cotton. China kept exporting large amounts of grain when there wasn't enough to feed its own people. People were starving to death. Between sixteen and twenty-seven million people died as a direct result of the famine in 1959. This was proportionately worse than the disaster in the Soviet Union under Stalin.

The failure of the Great Leap and the disastrous famine, which accompanied it, placed further strain on the authority of central government. At the center of power, there was resentment and criticism of Mao Zedong. But, Peng Dehuai, who made the strongest and clearest criticisms of Mao, forced a choice between himself and Mao. Peng was dismissed and Mao continued to hold immense prestige as leader of the revolution despite his many faults since then. His perhaps greatest fault was not allowing other points of view. If Mao got an idea, for better or worse, it became law. Often times his ideas were simplistic and shortsighted and they form the foundation of all the problems China is facing today.

Letter #15 from your student, Robert

Dear American Teacher,

In 1958, the Great Leap forward began. Everybody lay awake all night in fear or did not even go home, but continued to work. Most people were into steel making. I helped improve a machine, so called "Steelmaking." The scrap iron was cast into the indigenous furnace, also real iron or steel was melted and out poured steel with only the need to declare numerals. Within the Iron and Steel Company scrap iron was found everywhere. If people could not find enough in their homes, they might steal some from the iron works. There was a great problem in that people can only use their kettles as scrap iron once and the same with the use of their tables and benches as fuel. There was a limit to what was available and what people could produce.

At the end of this year I discovered that there was no more flour or rice, but only maize pellets that were big and tough and hard to swallow. As for other dishes, there was little to eat. Only at the Spring Festival could we get some meat. I remember that in the Spring Festival of 1959, we were also granted one ticket to buy an orange. My shoes were worn out and I did not have enough money to buy leather shoes. I hoped to buy gym shoes, but I could not get any. I found that we could not buy much of anything.

At this time, our party was immersed in great debate and division. Mao held the power and arranged for Peng Dehuai, who had criticized The Great Leap, to take some blame for its failure. He was dismissed.

Except for great steel making, we wrote many Da Zi Bao day to night, the one who wrote the most was a hero.

Sincerely, Robert

My first semester of teaching was soon over. The teacher's classes ended early because the Chinese teachers need the most time at the end of a semester because of the way they teach. The Chinese pattern of teaching involves having weeks of lectures and reading and then one big final exam that provides the grade for the entire course. The most time usually is needed to grade the exams.

By the time the semester was over, I had spent hours of time with Robert and his family. I knew that there was much more to tell. I was planning on traveling the entire summer to Beijing, the Three Gorges, Xian and as many other places as I could arrange.

I asked Robert to continue writing over the summer.

PART THREE:

ROBERT'S LIFE IN CHINESE LAOGAI

Editorial comment:

The words in Part Three were written by Robert during the summer. When I returned I was surprised at how much he had written. I was also shocked at some of the things he said. I had not understood how bad his experiences were until I read the details myself. Please prepare yourself for this last part, which has many brutal, gross and heartbreaking sections.

Robert and I spent hours in China verbally going over some of the things that he said to make sure that I understood them. At times we both sat with tears streaming down our faces. Unfortunately, we didn't have enough time to go over everything. There are some sentences that I still do not understand and so I left them with the hopes that his words would communicate best what he meant even though I wasn't sure what that was.
Now I wish he had written more, described things in greater detail and that we had spent more time pouring over his meaning. Once I returned to the U.S. I felt that I could not directly ask him questions for fear of the authorities finding out what we were doing and it would put him or worse, his teenage daughter in peril.

I tried to keep Robert's words as he wrote them, but I needed to make some changes in this section, especially in sequencing. Often times he would tell me of a certain situation and then go to the conclusion. Later he would go back and fill in the details as he remembered them. His thoughts were not always chronological. Sometimes he would remember a detail that he had forgotten and add it in the middle of what he was currently telling me.
I want to assure you that I have spent months going over his text to make sure that it is both understandable to you, the reader, and yet as close as possible to Robert's exact words and meanings.

Chapter One:

The Jinquan Iron and Steel Company in NW China (1960)

In April 1960, as further punishment, I was assigned to Jinquan Iron and Steel Company in northwestern China. It had just been established as a steel base. To get there, we traveled by train from northeast Anshan to northwest Jinquan, and it took four long days and nights. On the train we slept on a wide bed made to hold a number of people. But more people had to fit on the bed than it was made for and before long we all had lice. As the train went in a westward direction from Zhengzhou pass to Xian, it was obvious how the soil got poorer and poorer. Jinquan was at a distance of 10km beyond the Great Wall through the Jiayn Strategic Pass. It was a boundless stretch of the Gobi Desert. Sand and cobble were all over. There was essentially no water except for a little water and grass at a high altitude around the Jiayn Stratigic Pass. Beyond the Pass we could not see any green, but only light brown of the loose dirt and sand.

During our travel we saw several examples of the horror that was taking place in China at this time. After a brief stop, we discovered a boy outside the train, holding on to the door. He shivered with cold and was very hungry. We felt that we had to bring him into the carriage and give him food or he might drop off the train and be killed. Unfortunately there was little to spare because we had been given so little to eat. He had only what was given by the self-sacrificing ones. After he gathered whatever he could, he had even less than I had to eat.

At a stop to get off the train in Lanzhou, we were able to wash ourselves, but it was in yellow silt water. We saw what was unheard of in the 1950's, people trying to snatch food out of someone's hands while they were eating. The Jinquan town is at a distance 20 li (2 li=1 km) from base. On the way there we saw a group of children wearing only thin shirts and no trousers. Even a thirteen or fourteen year old girl did not have clothing to cover herself to be decent. In April, in the great northwestern area of China, it is still winter. We did not know how these children were surviving in the bitter cold, especially at night.

When we finally arrived at our work destination our first task was to build simple crude houses for us to live in. Many laborers also were made to dig a channel to plant trees. They had to draw water from a distance of 2 km from the Beida River. This was backbreaking work. With conditions such as this, neither people nor trees could survive. On May 1, which is International Labor Day, a holiday in China, we all hoped to get some meat from the government, but as often happened in these hard times, we were disappointed.

In October, I was assigned to work in the mine because it was the most arduous work. Jingtie Mountain is at a distance 20 li from base. We traveled by truck through the mountain range on a winding mountain dirt road. At the top of the mountain, which was a very high altitude, I developed a headache and severe congestion, which didn't leave for several weeks.

The day after we arrived at the mine, I realized the place where we were located was actually quite beautiful. Brown and violet mountain peaks, sparkling in the bright sun, surrounded us. The pass through which the Beide river flowed was an angry torrent with a temperature of 10 degrees C below zero. This river rolls thunderously on for a thousand li and we heard the roar all day and night long. A very strange thing happened at midday, it became dark. The sun hid behind a high mountain peak for two hours and then finally exposed itself again with bright wonderful light.

Next our task was making briquettes to warm ourselves. Our team drew the soil from the opposite bank and carried it by sling to us. Then we joined it with water and fine coal, making it into briquettes.

The food that we were given was very poor. Each person was given a grain coupon, but there was never enough to eat for all the hard labor that we were doing. We were all going hungry, and slowly, but surely starving to death. We were told to dig camel grass, which is a kind of shrub with a root that is found in the desert. Only camels will eat it. This was a vast territory with sparse camel grass. It was so sparse that one day we couldn't even find any. It also was bad because the grass tasted so bitter. We had to grind it into powder, which needed to steep in lukewarm water over night to get rid of the bitter taste. Then we had to dry it in the sun, mix it into grain powder and make it as steamed buns. The buns were bigger than we usually had, so psychologically it felt like we were eating more. We might also get half of a steamed egg or some edible seaweed once in a while.

Several days before this Spring Festival, I received an order to go back to the base. I traveled alone under the escort of a reliable party member and we went by tractor. It took an entire day and a night. When I got to the Jinquan base I realized the temperature was more than 20 degrees C below zero. I wore only a cotton-padded overcoat and lying on the tractor bed I shivered uncontrollably with cold. Frequently I ran, following the tractor to keep warm. As we passed, I saw a man sitting under the tree beside the mountain slope. It seemed that he was laughing, but then, in horror, I realized that he was dead. In such severe cold, you must push on with your journey even if you are cold and hungry. You can never sit down when you are tired because if you do, you may be like him and never get up.

My companions who left at a later time were less fortunate than I and had to walk on foot for two weeks through the mountains to get to Jinquan base. There were several posts on the winding mountain path with tents where people could rest, warm themselves by the fire and get water. One man after another would drop on the way, but it could not be allowed for one to stay down because that would imply certain death.

Things were getting worse all over. There was no longer a truck at the mine. There also was no food. That's how things stood at this terrible moment. At first when we arrived we had felt full and strong and warmly enough dressed that we had hopes of surviving. But, life now looked grim and hopeless. We were always cold, hungry and exhausted.

When I returned to the base, I first discovered that all the people there were getting fat despite not having enough food. It was confusing and strange. Then I was told that the condition is called dropsy. With dropsy, you suffer from hunger and as a product of deficient nourishment the body retains water.

Secondly, I found that people were in terrible condition when they needed to have a bowel movement. People were always crying with great pain when defecating. They were suffering from severe constipation. No stool could leave the body regardless how hard they pushed. People would have to dig the feces from their anus by hand. People had been eating only the camel grass steamed buns made with milling, sorghum with its husk. We very seldom had vegetables and there was absolutely no oil or fat to lubricate the body. We were eating so much fiber, but had no way to lubricate it out of the body. I suspected that I also might get dropsy and constipation, like the others. My only question was, how long would it take.

Indeed, the constipation started soon, but the dropsy did not come. Only one week after I had gotten to the base, the condition of my bowel movements became painful. Our lavatory was a cover over a hole in the ground in the field. There was much red excrement and bloodstain on the ground. Because it was so cold, 20 degrees below zero, the excrement quickly became very hard and there was no stink. A person could walk on it. I preferred to defecate on open ground. Oh, the pain made it feel as if I had a serious illness. I took deep breaths and controlled my diaphragm, but my excrement still stopped up my anus. I thought with the pain that this is perhaps like the cramps a woman has at the time of her menstrual period or at childbirth. People would cry so loudly and I was now among them. At 20 below zero in about half an hour I could dig the excrement bit by bit from my anus. From this time on I knew what a big space was found from rectum to anus. Originally I thought there was a small direct pipe from the rectum to the anus. But digging out each little bit made it seem so large.

It was one month since I had returned to base and I had not gotten dropsy. Perhaps it was because my sister had sent me a baked sweet potato in a grain ration from Shijiazhuang. She always knew what to send.

During this month workers lived relatively carefree and leisurely with no work except removing their stool. We would lie on the bed and talk about every matter or play poker. We sat around a fire to get warm every day. Only we were constantly hungry with so little to put into our mouths and such great pain to get anything out the other end.

American people may not understand or be able to imagine what such severe starvation is like. 12.5 kg to 20 kg of food each month is not enough to survive. You might try it, even for just a day or a short time. Have no meat, no grains, no vegetables and of course no fruit, only a bit of salted greens or greens with no salt, every day served in hot water, as a soup. The water actually filled us the most. Technical personnel, meaning those who do no physical exertion got 12.5 kg/ month and workers who did physical labor got 20 kg/month. After even a few days of such an experiment you will see how much food a person needs to survive and how not having it not only effects physical functioning, but so greatly more psychological functioning.

The Spring Festival was coming again. For over one year we had been living under such terrible conditions. We had no hope for meat because there was no meat anywhere to be had. But the Communist Government sent us white wheat flour for traditional steamed buns.

Some people could not handle the constant feeling of emptiness. It affects one psychologically and spiritually. You begin to feel as small and inconsequential as the food we got to eat. In order to experience the feeling of being full, young workers would sometimes use the entire month's grain coupon in a short period of time. Then they would totally starve with nothing to eat for the rest of the time. It didn't seem to matter that this was a very dangerous thing to do to one's health. And once the starvation begins it is hard to remember the brief good feelings of being full. Nothing seemed to matter except survival and some days when it was especially cold and dreary, death seemed that it could be a welcome escape.

Sometimes people would try to steal grain coupons. Someone stole my grain coupon one month. I knew who stole it, so I informed the security section. I knew that I would die if I had no food for a month. To my surprise the section chief reprimanded me. He said that I should not bother to report my problems, but that I should have vigorously grabbed the thief and taken care of it myself. I actually felt too weak to chase the man and probably fight with him. I shared all this with some others who slept near me and we finally approached the man as a group and regained my coupons.

One day a truck arrived at our base and people got on to unload the cargo. They soon discovered a dead young man. When did he climb in? Did he die of cold? Did he die of hunger? Or was it most likely a combination of the two? Regardless, it was a horrible sight to see one so young, dead. It seemed so meaningless.

CHAPTER TWO:

MOVED TO XIAN (1961)

In March of 1961 we were dispersed in an emergency because there was no food in Jinquan Iron and Steel Co. A part of our group went to Xinjiang, another to Jiag Xi and my group went to Xian.

Everyone was given a 1 kg flat cake made of maize flour. This was to be our food for the trip. We were fed in the freight train like domesticated animals seated on the floor. This kind of train would start and then stop, then travel for awhile and stop again. It was constantly brief travel followed by brief stops, but no one would know when or why. No time or consideration was given for bodily functions and it posed a great trouble. The male sex could urinate out of the door. That was for us very simple. But the females had the greatest difficulty. The women would completely surround the door and somehow hold the woman in balance out of the door. When the train stopped almost all the people jumped off in order to defecate. But, if the train started again as it often did without notice, we might have to quickly climb on carrying our trousers. There was no time for decency or modesty. We were in fear that we might be shot if we did not make it back on the train. It was not a possibility to use our stops as an escape except to death. A man with a rifle was usually insight.

After two days and nights we arrived in Langzhou and discovered that a young worker had died. He actually died from excessive eating. He felt so hungry that he ate all of his 1 kg maize flour cake at once and then drank a lot of water. It filled his digestive system to the point that the food could not be digested. When we got to Langzhou his body was sent to the hospital, as if to save him, but it was already too late when we had discovered him. The same type of unexpected death happened on the next leg of our train ride. But to keep from possibly having the body dumped off the train along the way, we propped up the body as if he were sleeping. After one more day and night we got to Xian and we acted like it was a new discovery of another dead young worker.

At Xian we were combined with the Xian Metallurgical Machine Works as a capital construction section. Xian had much food, but it was expensive. We used all of the little money we had accumulated to buy food. It felt so good and we were so content having a full sensation in our stomachs, a little more strength to function and more hopeful spirits.

Life seemed so much better having food to eat.

Chapter Three:

An Unbelievable Trip
to Shanghai in 1961

In Xian the summer temperature rose to 40 degrees C. The heat was unbearable. A female office worker at our capital construction section came to count up the number of people who were going home to visit families. I asked with little certainty, but great hope in my heart if I could go home to visit my family. This girl office worker with the best of intentions asked the secretary for instructions. I was so fortunate that he was a good person. He said: why not? It was so unexpected that I could hardly believe it for days. I arranged with my Shejiazuang sister to go to Wuhan to meet my brother. He had graduated from a maritime college in 1954. We, brothers and sister, hadn't seen each other for several years.

Our meeting was so wonderful and filled us with such comfort that I almost was able to forget the suffering of hunger. My sister even had brought an enamel washbasin, which was very hard to purchase at the time. It seemed like a real treasure. Life was getting better than I had, for a long time, dreamed it could be.

Soon my sister, brother and I were traveling together down the Changjiang River to Shanghai by ship. It suddenly seemed so normal compared to what I had been experiencing. It was very confusing and unbelievable.

Then when we got to Shanghai, wonder of wonders I met my fiancee whom I had not seen or had contact with for three long years. Beyond belief, she said that she still loved me and told me what had happened to her in these three years. She then said that two university graduates were seeking her hand in marriage. They had been her schoolmates. One was the secretary of their Communist Youth League. But she said that she doesn't like a full face of Marxism-Leninism. The other one was from a different quarter. He showed consideration for her and now they were good friends. Because of these other men and the one man's position, I had to see her in secrecy. These two schoolmates came to see her every Sunday. Sometimes they both were there close to the same time. The second one would arrive at the front door and she would ask the first one to sneak away from the rear door. Both she and the other man were in fear of the Communist Party secretary. She did not know how to refuse his interest. I saw both of the men from a chink in the door of her bedroom where I was hiding. She comforted me with her love to try to set my mind at rest. But after three years, now meeting again naturally my feelings were not clear and I was not certain of how she really felt. This time when I went back to Xian, her father fulfilled his task of giving us official permission to be engaged and we were able to write directly to each other.

The entire country was in a state of hunger. The Communist Party could not do enough to improve people's lives. Since 1960 no initiatives or movements came from the party and political affairs seemed to have gotten "flabby." In reality, we had enough trouble to deal with the lack of food and our own survival. We did not need political directives for additional harassment.

In 1962, after sufficient time had passed, I was able to remove my rightist label. I had hopes that this would greatly improve my life.

On New Year's Day I was again able to go to Shanghai. I stayed with my fiancée's family. After I arrived I was taking a bath after the journey and enjoying being in a comfortable home and a bathtub. I had inserted the electric heater plug in the socket. When I was in the bathtub carelessly my left hand touched the heater and I got an electric shock. There seemed to be a leakage of electricity. My left hand held the heater and could not let go. My heart felt a gust of spasm. The stove began to tilt toward the bathtub. I could clear-headedly tell that I was in grave danger. Just in that time my heart shrank and I felt in a fit, but this was only for seconds. Then my hand loosened its grip. What had saved me? I found out that one of the poles of the plug had fallen off. It was just a line pole because the electric wire was too short. How happy I was to have survived a possible tragedy, but I thought that if I had died a meaningless death, people would laugh at me. People would also think of the injustice because I had just removed the right-ist label and might miss a better future.

CHAPTER FOUR:

MY ROMANCE SLOWLY
ENDS FROM 1962 TO 1965

This was a time when the political atmosphere of the whole nation tended to relax, but my personal situation still had not shown improvement, as I had hoped. Even though I had officially removed the rightist label, I was still considered a rightist and I encountered discrimination against me. My wages still had not returned to normal, but had only attained the level of a new graduate (50 yuan). This made my fiancée's parents very disappointed in me. They thought that I still had not returned to normal after removing the label and they were no longer supportive of our love.

After this visit when I had returned to Xian, she wrote to me and suggested that things were not working as we had hoped and she wished to part company with me. It was impossible for me to return to Shanghai to try to change her mind. She said that she still loved me, but we are more like brother and sister. From then on she never wrote to me again. It seemed impossible for me to comprehend. I was totally confused because, in private, she treated me as warmly as usual. When I had to go back she said quietly that she would love me forever. I had to return to Xian, but she said that I should set my mind at rest about our relationship. However, not a long time after being back in Xian, I received a letter again saying that she must part company with me. This time she said that we could only be friends. She did not write again.

The one year I had to wait to return to Shanghai seemed like a very long time and the details of the meaningless work and physical discomforts are too boring to describe. In the summer of 1964, I went to Shanghai. This time I knew that I could not set foot in her home. I called her to come to my oldest sister's home. She came, but appeared distressed, although she embraced me as usual. We saw each other as much as possible, but these times were all in private. However, shortly after arriving back in Xian, I received another letter from her asking that we part company. She said that we could not even be friends. Now I fully knew that there would be no next time. I had lost a fine girl and my heart was broken, but I could not give up. I wanted to see her once more and speak clearly. But I had to prepare to break off the relationship forever.

In 1964 the famine was alleviated. With the country being out of a crisis, the political atmosphere was tending to deteriorate again. The "four clean movement" was coming. I also lost confidence that I could ever shift my job to Shanghai.

In the beautiful spring of 1965, I gathered all the gifts and souvenirs she had given me. I had slippers for ten years that she had embroidered and made with her own hands. There were it seemed, a thousand letters that she had written to me. My ten-year long love story had ended for good. When I went to Shanghai I called her and told her that I had brought back all the souvenirs she had sent to me. She was not willing to meet me. (Sixteen years later she told me that it was her father who told her to not meet me. If she had, she felt that she would never leave me. But, by then, it really didn't matter.) She asked me to leave all the things at my sister's house and she would get them and also return all of my gifts later.

I could not give up. I remember that it was a Monday, a radiant and enchanting spring scene after about 2 o'clock when I went to her work unit. I stayed outside, but paced up and down. I was too early and she would not be through with work until 5 PM. What could I do until then? I subconsciously walked along the clean and tidy street and crossed to the opposite side of the street. I saw that there was running water under the little bridge and red flowers and green willows. I imagined that it was such a charming place for us to meet and talk. I strode over the running water, across the bridge, and without thinking I went in a gate. There was more delightful scenery in the compound. I went on and suddenly discovered that I was in a production unit. There was another gate in front of me. Just as I went out of the gate with an uneasy feeling in my heart, I was called to halt by a guard. They took me to their security section. It seems that this was a secret unit. They asked me, as if I were a spy, "Where do you come from?" Where is your work unit? What do you want?" I replied that I came from Xian to see my fiancee and she is in a medical institute nearby here and I must get there by 5 o'clock.

After half an hour the comrade of the security section came back and spat out one terrible sentence, "You are a rightist!" But, he then allowed me to leave. I waited outside of the institute. I knew that she knew that I was waiting for her. At 5 o'clock sharp she walked haltingly with a girl friend coiled on one arm and brushed me aside. I followed her to get on the bus. It was especially crowded. I had no courage to follow her any longer. I felt that she had brought humiliation upon me. It made me blush with shame. I seemed to have become a rogue stalking a female. I went from being a fiancée to being a stalker. How I wished I could lie down under the bus suddenly. But there was a crowd of people completely surrounding me. It seemed that they heaved a sigh. Would she feel any compunction? Suicide in China can be an honorable death under the right conditions. But it was inevitable that the Communist party would not take any pity on me. I was a common person and a rightist. If I were to do something like that they would feel justified in labeling me as an unworthy person. I became reconciled to settle my life by perhaps dying of a broken heart aided by starvation. But, after some time I decided to live because I believed that she would be bound to face me one day at last in the future. Even that sad hope made me want to live.

CHAPTER FIVE:

THE FAMINE PASSES BY 1965

That the famine could pass so quickly was quite unexpected. I remembered back in 1960, there were many apprentices who came from the Gansu Province countryside and they had gone home to visit their families. They came back to tell that the famine would not pass for eight to ten years because all the farm cattle had been butchered, so there could be no reproduction. Also the supply of seeds for future crops had been eaten.

But, unexpectedly since 1963, people found that food was slowly progressively increasing. Pork began to be even more available than before 1957. You could buy pork without a coupon. It seemed that the terrible famine had passed after only three years.

What was the reason? It is simple and, of course, the Communist Party would want to take the credit. People could survive in this time if they lay down and did nothing. People can't work when starving. The Communist Party should not poke their noses into this. Peasants can tillage by themselves. Our peasant compatriots saved our country from the dead edge and brought it back alive. From here I concluded that the hardworking and mighty Chinese people made out the great strength of masses. Originally, we Chinese people all along were celebrated for our hard work and diligence. The price we paid would be much more. We left our native areas. We worked all-day and attended meetings at night with no days off. We worked conscientiously several tens of years, when one pair, a man and wife could not support a child, if they were lucky enough to be allowed to marry.

Chapter Six:

The Great Cultural Revolution in 1966

In May of 1966, "The Great Cultural Revolution" started. At the outset, the spearhead was directed at me and "the four kinds of elements," which included landlords, rich peasants, counter-revolutionaries and "bad elements," plus rightist for a total of five. It was actually "five kinds of elements." The titles were confusing, but the intention of the movement was not.

To begin with, we were put under public surveillance and little movement was allowed. Afterwards, from a high level of the Communist Party an instruction was given. At this time there was a switch in victims and the goal was to uncover persons in authority who it was said, "took the capitalist road." So, we "dead pigs" as we were called, temporarily averted a catastrophe.

Soon afterwards at my place of work many persons in authority were "uncovered." Many were section chiefs and work directors who had somehow angered the workers beneath them, some wrongly and some rightly. They were all locked in a cowshed. The Secretary of Capital Construction Section named Guo controlled them all and actually worked together with the "five kinds of elements" to uncover other "guilty" people. It was a psychological strategy that people, especially children, often use today, that if I can focus attention on other guilty people maybe it will be forgotten how guilty I am considered.

Guo was most cruel to feeble men. He always put politics in motion and used the despicable act of drawing in one faction of workers to report and rat-out another. He always framed a case against another. He depended on people turning in and punishing others in order to secure a promotion or to make some money.

He went from being a section secretary to become the director of the political department of our company. With the deepening of the "great Cultural Revolution", groups of rebels were often divided in two. The ends were played against the middle. They ferreted out leaders who the other group wanted to save, and they would guard and protect leaders who the other group was to ferret.

After time the tension was so great that people had to resort to violence. They held lances made of steel tubes to capture a part of the workshops and living quarters. It was most frightening to see the animal-like glare in their eyes, so much like a tiger eyeing its prey. At this time it constantly happened that people would snatch weapons from troops on duty in various parts of our city. After all, even the soldiers had to close their eyes occasionally.

The biggest violence in Xian occurred on the crossroads right near our company. At night on September 1, 1968, two groups of city workers held a decisive battle. They used both firearms and lances. In the early morning of September 2nd, corpses were found everywhere. Ten people had been killed, eight of whom belonged to our company.

As to the whole nation, even more violence happened due to Jiangqing (Mao's wife), Wang Hong Wen, Zhang Chu Qiao and Yao Wen Yuan, also known as the "four people's faction" or "gang of four." They rode roughshod on whom they wanted to criticize and denounce, whom ever they wanted to kill. Even Lu Shao Qi could not make his escape from them.

After this rebel group the spearhead was directed at the "black nine kinds of elements." So now the persecuted groups increased to nine kinds, including bourgeois elements, etc. This was aimed even more directly at punishing me.

First, I was accused of compelling my close friend to become a bad element. Bricklayers struggled against time every night until midnight. They forced him to tell of my words and deeds. One night it was 1 o'clock when he finally reached our living quarters. Suddenly I heard him say in the next room—"Long live Chairman Mao." I ran out of my room to his room. I got there in time to see my friend, this bricklayer, jumping out of the third floor window. He did not die but was maimed (his back was broken). Fortunately, he was sent to a home in Shanghai to recuperate. The Shanghai neighborhood committee at once kept watch on him and did not ask why. In that time we often were ferreted out by other shops, which were criticizing and denouncing us. At times they would use a brass instrument and put a high cap (dunce cap) to parade us through the streets to expose us before the enemy—the public. Because I have a strong character I always readily confessed my offenses to them so I had to endure untold suffering in that time of numerous parades and humiliation.

Before 1969 at my work unit, three persons had been punished to death. Two of them were an old married couple who were hung by their necks. The third was a graduate from the University at Wuxi in the class of 1952. He had gone to Anshan Iron and Steel Company with us. He had become a close friend of mine. He was beaten to death, but they told lies about how he died. They said that he died from jumping from a fire escape staircase outside of the shop. Around 2 AM, two people were on duty at the metal processing shop and they heard many footsteps outside. They saw several people drag a man and throw him under the fire escape staircase to make it look like he had jumped to his death. In the morning they told his wife to come to claim his body. After his wife saw his body, she left without saying a word and showed no tears. She was afraid that if she had wept, it might seem that she could not bear to part from him and she too might have "an accident."

Chapter Seven:

The Most Intense Time of the Cultural Revolution in 1970

In 1970 there was launched the "one beat and three oppose" movement. This was the most frenzied period in the great Cultural Revolution. The county government was allowed to execute people by shooting and did not have to report to the higher authorities for approval.

In March of 1970, I had been locked in a type of basement. It actually was an air defense air-raid shelter that had been dug at the time. This basement was under the air defense command of our work unit. It was very simple and crude. A person had to go through a little iron door, take a step down through another little door you will enter the basement. It was about 40 meters square and dark. There was a lamp hung on the ceiling, which was 3 meters from the ground, but it was always turned off. It was also very damp. When you adapt your eyes to the dark you could see small lines of light coming from a crack in the upper brick wall. It felt like there was a shortage of oxygen. I felt like I was going to suffocate. I climbed on a bed type structure and drew in deep breaths to calm myself. I was living without light and without hearing any sound. After about two weeks I felt that I would go insane. Breathing seemed to be harder and harder, but it was probably from lack of exercise.

One night I heard a sound from above. It was the opening of the iron door. I heard footsteps of many people. The door had been held shut with iron chains, which I heard being removed. The basement door opened. Now that I could see this was just like a ghastly prison. The electric torch projected a beam of light. Five or six persons came in with a man who was the leader, but I did not know any of them. The leader looked around and asked what the voltage of the ceiling lamp was. I answered 220 volts, but at 3 meters high I said that I could not reach it.

I had at an earlier time told my brother who was now in Nanjing that I did not think that I would under any circumstances take my own life. I said that if ever I died in this situation, I probably was murdered, regardless what officials tell you.

After I had been locked up for 2 weeks, on March 28th I was escorted out of the basement and was taken to a stage in an open square to be criticized and denounced. The square was thronged with a dense crowd. An old colleague of mine, Mr. Zhou, stood at the corner of the stage. He had been married and divorced. He later married a young woman who was just eighteen years old. He often beat her and greatly mistreated her. She tried to escape many times, but he was always able to bring her back. At last she jumped out of a window and killed herself. Then Zhou slept with an official's wife and as many women as he could. Because of his sexual behavior he had been cast in the cowshed as an obviously undesirable person.

We stood on different sides of the stage. After a violent barrage of criticism and denouncement, high officials who wore military uniforms took action against us. First, they bound Zhou's hands behind him. Then with the rope harnessed around his neck, they drew it tighter. I could see how his face showed extreme distress. Then they bound me also. The rope was harnessed around my neck. They drew it tight. My God, this was such a surprise physical attack on me. The rope tightened.

Then they dragged Zhou from the stage into the square and into a truck. I was now laying on the stage alone. Three men grabbed me and carried me through the air like an airplane and threw me into the same truck. We were on our knees and if we lifted our heads they would punch us back down. The rope was so tight that I could not breathe and each time I was hit I saw stars and felt I would go unconscious.

The truck started driving and after about 15 minutes we got to the branch of the police station. I wondered how long we would have to stay in the truck. It felt like we could die of suffocation. I heard a policeman say to the Red Guards that they had been working hard that night. We were removed from the truck. The policeman lifted our faces and looked at us. We were moved to stand against the wall. The policeman asked someone to get a towel, a quilt and an enamel mug. I was told to sign my name to the credential for being arrested. I still had trouble with my breathing and sweat continued to pore from my forehead. The policeman asked why I continued to gasp and sweat, but I would think that he could figure out the reason. Later a man in the same prison said that the bruise from the rope remained on my neck for more than two months.

Chapter Eight:

Sent to Prison in 1970

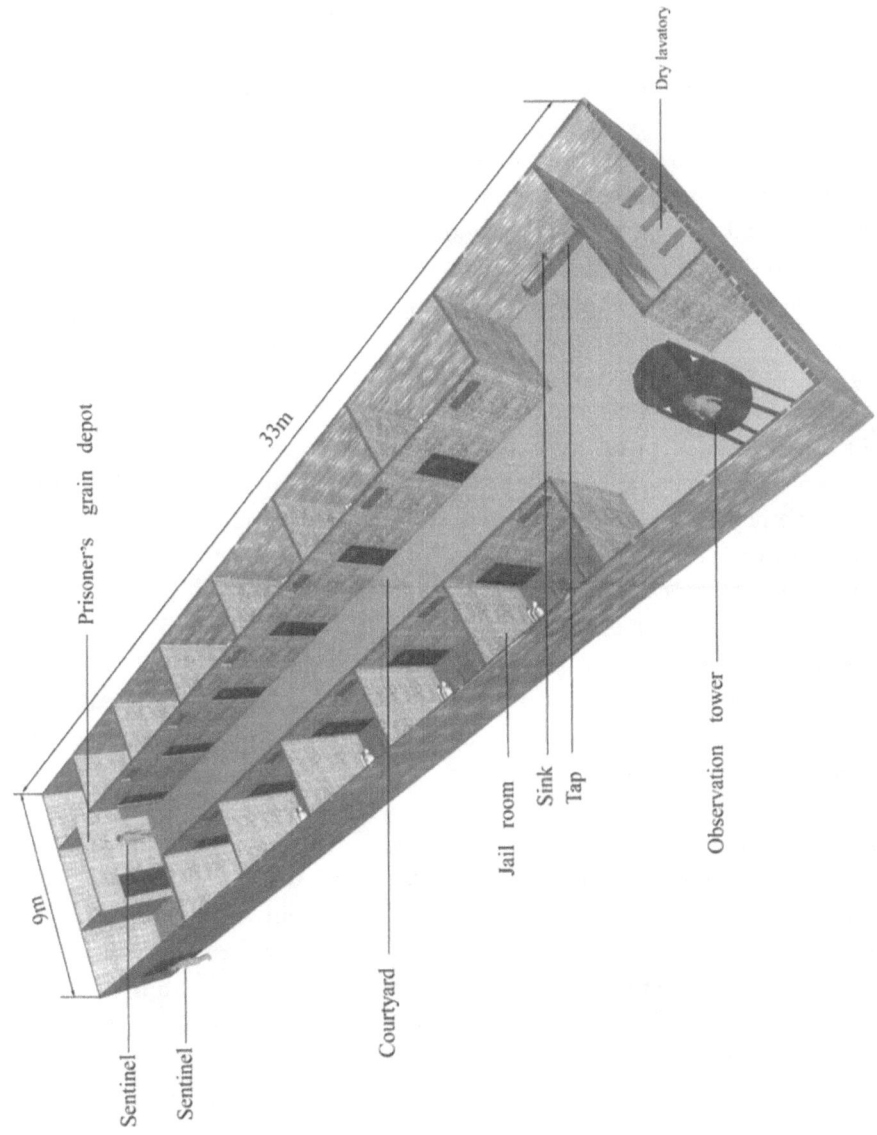

Dry lavatory

Prisoner's grain depot

33m

9m

Jail room

Sink

Tap

Courtyard

Observation tower

Sentinel

Sentinel

That night I was driven to a prison. The prison had a courtyard with a skylight in the center. It was lined with eleven prison cells. On one end there was an area for storing prisoners' food and on the other side a lavatory and water tap. It all was very clean and tidy, but smelly. When I first arrived at the prison I thought that I had arrived at a bathhouse. The smell was awful and had the damp unique odor peculiar to a bathhouse. It did not seem like a prison because of the bright sunshine.

Twice a day, at 9AM and 4 PM we are allowed outdoors to relieve ourselves and get fresh air in our cells. This was called by the guards, "Let in the fresh air." Each room had two large metal pails, one is for green soup and the other is for boiling water. There was also a basket for steamed corn bread. After we were allowed out and had let the fresh air into our cells, we were given a meal.

Prisoners were barefoot and had to sit on the wide bed for 16 people. The wide bed was 1.8 meters wide and 4 meters in length and only 20 cm off the floor. The room was 4 meters by 2.5 meters, so there was little floor space. At night sixteen men slept on the bed opposite each other, head to feet. The other four men had to sleep on the floor. Two men had to share a padded blanket. During the day we all sat on the bed and could not move. We were supposed to think about our crimes. There were also two metal pails that were used as urinals.

When the guards came, the prisoners formed a tight line against the wall. When the lock was opened and the guard yelled, "let in the fresh air" the prisoners made a nervous rush out the door. We must hurry or receive a beating. We rushed out the door to the water tap in the yard. I would stay sandwiched between others. There was only one tap so the prisoners would wash their hands at random. The lavatory was near-by. It was neat and tidy, but smelly. Everyday there were two prisoners on duty to turn over the heap of manure. They also sandwiched themselves between people to clean the urine stool under the tap. Then we were allowed to use the lavatory. If there was a mean guard we had only 1 minute to defecate. If there was a good guard we had a little more time. Then the order was given to "return." Everyone immediately formed a line and went back to the cells. It was a very tense atmosphere. The person who marched at the head of the column always took the food that was laid out by the door. In these seconds he might steal a little extra food without anyone seeing him, but it had to be done quickly. One day when I got in the cell there was no food left for me. I asked for some and was given the corn bread, but no soup or boiled water.

There was a little window in the door for the squad leader to watch that the prisoners did not move. At the top of the wall was an open window allowing in bright sunlight. This was such an improvement over the damp basement with only a crack of light where I had been kept all alone. It was a great improvement to have cellmates, except that there were too many for the amount of room we had.

The first night by 8:30 everyone had fallen asleep. I was lying against the wall thinking of the woman I had loved years before. It was better that we had broken off the relationship rather than for her to know I was in prison. I was happy that the relationship had ended. A little bedbug crawled down the wall and I killed it with my finger. Then another came and another. In the 30 minutes before I fell asleep, I killed perhaps 80 bed bugs. Within two to three days my body was covered with lice. My waist was one bite beside the other. I itched day and night. I was constantly tired from dealing with the lice and bedbugs. It was impossible to sleep deeply.

Chapter Nine:

Becoming Very Sick

One day a young man who was only seventeen years old and sleeping at the other end of the bed was suddenly taken ill. He had a high fever and he groaned as if in pain. I feared that I too would become ill because ever since I was a child I had not been strong. If I saw someone else sick, it seemed that I too would become ill. So, I became sick only two weeks after entering prison.

I lay on the floor with a heavy head. The ceiling was blurred and spinning. I don't know how many days passed. I was lying on the bed and suddenly heard, "let in fresh air." I quickly got up. Another prisoner laid prostrate on the floor for me to climb on his back. I asked him what he was doing. He replied that he had been carrying me out for ten days while I was unconscious. I decided that I now must be recovering from the illness. When a person is sick he often does not eat any food and the one who takes care of him is allowed to eat his food. This was the rule. When the guard yells "let in the fresh air" all prisoners, healthy or sick must leave the cell. My caretaker carried me out and put me up against the wall.

This time I went out by myself, but I was too tired to walk to the water tap. I leaned up against a close wall. I was given steamed corn bread, but in a twinkling it was stolen from where it lay on my chest. Some prisoners were outraged by the injustice. They gave the thief a scolding. Since I had been sick so long and had no nourishment I was so weak. For someone to steal my bread was heartless.

I asked the other prisoners how I had been able to manage since I had been unconscious for so long. They said that they had helped me get undressed for sleeping. But I was most puzzled how I could defecate since one must carefully place one's feet so as not to fall in. They said that somehow I had managed because I knew that I had to.

It was actually two months before I was completely recovered. I could not believe that I had survived such a severe illness.

In such a prison the first problem is getting enough food and next comes the crowding and then hygiene difficulties that can lead to illness and often death.

In 1970 from March 28 to November 15, I was in the Lianhu District Public Security Bureau. They stipulated that every prisoner must get 450 grams of grain in two meals each day. There was steamed bread of corn, maize gruel and husked Kaoliang, which is a Chinese food. Sometimes there would be two steamed breads or one bowl of husked Kaoliang with one bowl of soup. We got two ladles of boiled water each day. Some days there would be two bowls of maize gruel and no soup or water.

Although it said that 450 grams of food was to be given, something was deducted for being declared guilty. That full amount was only for prisoners doing strong labor. I think that many days I only received 250 grams. We always felt the agony of hunger and we would get very keyed up over food. All twenty bowls were laid out to distribute the food, which is not often equal. Two prisoners play a finger guessing game to determine the order of distribution. Each one puts out fingers and the total figure. Prisoners use a code for the sake of maintaining secrecy of the prisoners' identity. This prisoner would take the first bowl. The others were taken in the proper order. Therefore, if there were a broken bowl, it would appear there was no alternative, but to report it to the administrator because a broken bowl would be very difficult to use under such circumstances. We would get another bowl in about one week. The person who had the broken bowl would have to wait to the end to eat. He then would use someone else's bowl and only get what was left in the bucket. If possible we tried to keep the broken pieces of bowl to trim our fingernails. One time each month our heads were shaved and then the hair would grow back for a month.

The soup was so salty and there often was a layer of silt or seasoning at the bottom. We could have nothing remaining in our bowls. If you had soup or sediment remaining it seemed that you were given too much and next time you would get less. Greens soup was especially salty and there was so little water to drink. We always were thirsty, especially before we went to bed. It was almost too much to bear during the night. Being thirsty was more than you can stand until the next morning when it finally subsided. As you can tell, our nights were miserable.

The twenty bowls were washed with only one mug of water. The lack of hygiene often made us feel nauseated. We also hated how the time went too quickly when we were having a meal. We could never linger over a mouthful, but always had to gulp our food down quickly, without manners or even civility.

It was an interesting situation that in prison with little food, no one had stomach troubles. After a little time, we all became fine with our little digestion and no one ever had a stomachache. So, if you have a gastric disease, I suggest that you should spend several months of your life in the prison of the Chinese Communist Party. I assure you, you will be cured of your gastric disease. In the prison you wait for only two mealtimes a day. That was the only expectation that we had and the only thing we had to look forward to every day.

Who on earth has not suffered from hunger at sometime in his life? All have sometime experienced not having had a meal on time, waking up in the morning wanting to eat or you may even have been hungry for one day or perhaps two before pay day. You would call that hunger. But almost the entire Chinese population, who lived from 1960, knew unbelievable hunger and some starvation. We had to use grain coupons to buy food. Grain coupons were limited in number. It seems that no one had eaten his fill for years. I think that if you really want to know how real hunger feels you need to go to a prison of the Communist Party. I'm talking about the time during "The Great Cultural Revolution."

What about now in Chinese Communist Prison Camps, I do not know. Stay there several months and you will find out.

Prisoners can sometimes know what it is like to feel full. We often gathered four to five prisoners' food at one time giving it to one man to eat. Then you could experience what it is to be full. Unfortunately then you must go hungry for two or three whole days with nothing.

Chapter Ten:

An Example of Real Hunger

In order to express how the prisoners long to "eat," I will tell you a story that may make you sick to your stomach or perhaps you will burst into tears hearing it.

One day two old men were on duty during the time we left our cell to "let in the fresh air" and defecate. They had to turn over two heaps of manure and dump the closed bucket of stools into a pond. Then suddenly came the sound of "return." But, only one bucket was totally empty and the cover put on. They had to immediately return to the prison room. The guard went out of the room holding the door lock and gave each a hit on the head with the heavy lock and he kicked the last two men. They staggered into the room and one, losing his balance bumped one of the uncovered stools against a metal pail of maize gruel that had been put before the bed. A drop of night soil splashed down the metal pail of maize gruel, which was our next meal. This young man in a state of confusion bravely yelled out, "Something terrible has happened." He was thinking of just mixing it in the maize gruel. The other man yelled, "No." He had a better idea, to dredge up the night soil with a ladle. Then they distributed the maize gruel and we all ate it as if nothing terrible had happened. This experience of such great hunger and lack of pride will always be branded on my memory. How great was our need for nourishment!!

While in prison, I always regretted the years that I had not eaten breakfast, which I seldom did in my early life. One day at 5:00 AM the maize gruel had been set out the door. We saw its steam at daybreak and smelled it scent. We were all hungry and I would also say, greedy. I took an oath that day that if I were to survive prison, I would regularly take breakfast every morning and remember what all I had suffered and survived. Breakfast has been a good time for me, to daily look at my life and value the wonder of it all.

I, for some reason, often dreamed of eating shelled peanuts. Perhaps I wanted something to crunch and chew rather than the soft watery food that we got. I also dreamed of taking a bath and brushing my teeth. For the two years that I was in prison I did not bathe or change clothes. Since I had no family near by to help me, I had nothing except what I had with me when I was taken prisoner or had been given to me by others. When I came to prison I fortunately was wearing long underwear, which I was able to keep. In the summer when it got so hot I was able to make a loincloth from a towel. I still have this loincloth to remind me of what I have survived.

CHAPTER ELEVEN:

SEVERE CROWDING

Picture 1

In this time of being in prison, the other hardship we had to endure was the severe crowding. It was difficult and unpleasant during the daytime, but at night it is unbearable. I have said that there were sixteen persons on a wide bed and four other persons must sleep on the ground. There were two persons to one sleeping blanket. We were divided feet to head with every other two people sleeping opposite. One must sleep on one's side. Often times the crowding caused an exchange of blows.

It was most difficult if the man sleeping on one end of the room needed to go to the bucket on the other side to urinate. It was a hard path to follow. He must insert his feet in between the head and body and move very carefully. If he bumped into another, a dispute might be started. People tried so hard to not have to urinate at night.

We felt packed in tighter than sardines all the time. In addition, the prison stipulated that we were not allowed to tell each other our names. So we all used a code to tell each other our work unit and occupation. We were not allowed to talk. Prisoners had to sit up straight on the bed and could not make a sound. This was called "ideological remolding and self-criticism." If you were speaking or moving and the squad leader discovered you when he randomly opened the little window in the door, you would be punished. You might be ordered to stretch out your hands outside the small window and they would be struck. They also might have a rubber band put around your wrist. After sometime or if it happened too many times, the wrist would become cut or discolored from lack of circulation. You could receive a beating if it happened too often.

The guards had many ways to punish us. For example, one night two prisoners fought over a place on the bed. The squad leader punished them by making them stand for three hours without being able to sleep.

Every two weeks family members of the lucky ones were allowed to deliver things for prisoners, except no food was allowed to be brought in. The main item that was delivered was toilet paper, which made life so much better. Also cotton wadding was needed to create warmth when it was cold. Things were only allowed to come in, nothing could go out. If the family delivered a quilt in the winter, during the warm season the guards gave us a hard time because our prison room was so small and there was no place for storage. The supreme dread we strangely felt was having a family member deliver a quilt at the wrong time and it might disappear.

Family members of the lucky ones brought toilet paper every two weeks. My greatest need was for toilet paper. If my family had been there I know that they would gladly have sent me toilet paper, but I had no one to help me. At that time there were no coupons to buy toilet paper. I will not describe the discomfort and agony this caused, but you can perhaps imagine how terrible it could be.

At that time in China every household and person was registered. Then each person was given coupons for a certain weight of food according to their occupation and station. To buy any food a person had to have coupons, even for rice and cooking oil. A physical worker was allowed more food and rice than an office worker. Children were given coupons for a quantity of food according to their age. There were some people who were not registered for coupons, but were able to stay alive by getting coupons from others. The most common example of this were prostitutes who often received no coupons, but could be paid with coupons. Some unfortunate women were forced into prostitution in order to eat.

As additional punishment, a prisoner also might be sent to an administrator. The guards did not keep the key to the door of our cell. It was believed that if they were able to open the door at any time to come in and take prisoners out as they deemed necessary, they would beat, mistreat and eventually kill all the prisoners. The guards could be very cruel people. They could report you for various infractions and an administrator would come with the key to take you out. You would be handcuffed and taken away for an unknown and severe fate. The fear itself was often punishment enough.

There were all types of people in prison besides political prisoners. Evildoers of every hue were also put in prison. There were thieves, local ruffians, hoodlums, violators of labor contracts, quack sellers of tea, and supposed spies for Russia or America. What this meant is that if you knew a foreigner or had any contact with a foreigner it was assumed that you were a spy for that country. There became a list of the black nine kinds of elements. Like me the man who ferreted out antagonistic organizations in the "great cultural revolution." It was as if dragons and fish were all jumbled together. Outside is a big world and the prison is a little world. I saw and learned many many things in this little world that I had had no idea about before.

CHAPTER TWELVE:

A SENSELESS WASTE OF MY
LIFE AT FORTY

By this time I was forty years old. After I left the university I had only worked for one big company. A big company, I have been told, is different in China because here it is like a small city. We work and live in the same place which all has a wall around it. Often, for days on end we never left our area of perhaps a city block in America. I did not know what life might be like outside my company. I did not have any contact with society outside my company. I only had known the men who I worked with. But, in prison I saw people of every hue. There was a great dividing line between intellectual and non-intellectuals. Bad elements outside the prison also behaved badly in prison.

In prison, we all struggled with our plight, but some of us rallied together to struggle with the adverse circumstances. I tried to persuade people to show consideration for each other, but often it was a vain. We political offenders were mostly intelligent and well behaved. We were not punished as often with beatings, etc. unless, of course the guards had the time to spare and sensed that someone might be acting as if they were "better than" others.

In addition to hunger making us suffer, the cold was so terrible. Because the guards would not allow us to move around the cold seemed worse and could sink into our bones. In addition, we were always hungry and low on energy, so even if we could move we didn't feel like it. The hunger and cold together were a painful and sometimes deadly combination. Many of us had no padded clothes. Fortunately as a prisoner, I received one blanket, which I most often had draped over my shoulders. Whenever I found a good administrator I would always say that I needed padded clothes. Sometimes he would reply, "you bourgeois element."

But, the worst suffering was due to the senselessness of our lives. It often made us feel terrible misery. We looked forward to eating and "let in the fresh air" which happened twice a day. Otherwise our lives seemed most miserable because we could do almost nothing. It was such a senseless waste of time. I spent so many hours remembering my family members, going over past memories in great detail and then, of course, worrying and wondering how they were in the present. I would always dream of having a book to study so that I did not have to just sit and stare in space. Sometimes we were able to sneak learning experiences.

For example, there was a lecturer and engineer named Mr. Wu who had been an engineer at the Xi'an Electric Furnace Company. He had even studied abroad in his early years in Japan in the 1960s. He had worked in Shenjang where the Japanese were located in China. In the 1970s a famous Japanese man named, Gao Qi Da Zhi Zhu came to China to meet with a famous Chinese man named Liao Cheng Zhi. They agreed to meet in Beijing. Mr. Wu went to their Beijing hotel. He thought over the danger of this action. He used an alias. Now this "one beat, three oppose" movement included people who could be Japanese spies and he was cast into prison. We all learned much about electrical engineering with his widespread knowledge. We probed technology regularly in this respect. This way we made some use of our time when it was possible.

There also was a man locked up with me who knew Arabic. For two weeks I was able to study Arabic with him until we became afraid that someone might inform against us and so we gave up. There was a man with us who had been an interpreter for a leading USSR specialist. He was charged with being a revisionism spy. He was called a "Red Imp" which is a term of endearment in addressing a child and red means of the Communist Party. He was born into an early Communist family in Harbin. He followed the USSR specialist traveling back and forth between China and Russia in the 1950s and 60s. Frequently he was invited to stand on the Ti'an gate with Mao during festivals. He ate rare foods and had a big capacity for eating. After China and USSR turned against each other and stopped being friends, the Chinese showed him no mercy. He was cast into prison as a Russian Spy. He felt extreme hunger. He bartered a watch and woolen sweater for steamed corn bread.

I had said that food would be strictly forbidden to enter prison from the family members. But, they were allowed to send in one quilt with cotton wadding, one towel and one mug. Then it was added that a few bits of sugar ginger was allowed because it may prevent disease. I was fortunate that whenever a prisoner's family member carried something in, many times people shared it with me because they knew I had no one near-by.

I had been in prison here for six long months and my old mother, brothers and sisters who were in Shanghai and Guangzhou did not know for sure where I was. Many times I asked prison authorities to allow me to send a letter. Finally, one day they allowed me to write and two weeks later, my oldest sister sent me a parcel from Shanghai. It had a lot of toilet paper and several kilograms of sugar. Prison authorities only gave me part of the toilet paper and only about half of a kilo of sugar.

I felt much suffering when I thought about myself. But, other thoughts caused me to feel relief. As I looked back at that year when my fiancée wanted us to break-up, I now realized that it was for the best. I am afraid I could not bear the mental agony if we had married and then I was sent to prison. I would have felt more concern for her having her husband sent to prison.

Prisoners mostly talked about food and past times of good eating. Northeastern people talked about the special northeastern dishes, we southern people talked about our southern dishes and Xi'an people talked about their local dishes. The more we talked, sometimes, the more hunger we felt. Sometimes we literally drooled with envy over describing an especially delicious dish.

One day when a "good" administrator heard about our talk, he gave us a scolding. He said that we were as those in the "capitalist class". I agree that maybe "eating" is an enjoyment of capitalist class, but does that mean that the proletariat does not want to "eat" or does not have hunger or does not want to have simple pleasures of life.

This was one of my biggest mistakes, that I too often made comments and had sharp things to say when I should have been silent. In America, I think, I might be called a "smart Alec." This certainly could be called a bad quality of mine, but I feel that I have more than paid the price for it and regardless what the consequence, I have not learned to control myself. I have noticed that my American teacher is like me in that respect.

She often makes "smart Alec" comments, which to me seem very clever and funny. Of course she does not make comments about the Chinese Government or Communism. In America, it seems OK to say almost anything.

CHAPTER THIRTEEN:

CREATIVITY PREVAILS

There was a young prisoner who was particularly clever. We could not see outside our cell, but in ways we could replace our eyes with our noses and other senses. Usually before we heard "let in fresh air," the metal pails with food were put just beside the door. Prisoners would pretty well know what the meal was and especially if it was dry or liquid. We could tell by the sound when the metal pails were set down. We could sense if it was hot or cold by the presence of stream that we didn't actually see, but could feel or somehow sense. We could tell if it was salty or there was no salt by the subtle smell. We also picked up the slightest clues from everything around us.

The grain depot was near our room, and if at 5–6 o'clock PM we heard sounds in the grain depot, we knew that later we would be eating hushed gao-liangs. Although they tried to take everything from us so we had absolutely nothing, they could not take the use of our minds, our creativity and our imagination where anything could happen and everything could be allowed.

An example of what we could do is that we took a great deal of time to create the game of chess. White and black chess pieces were made with cloth. I learned how to play chess in prison. In those long stupid days, we played all kinds of games, but we had to be careful to play in such a location that the guards could not see. We played chess under the wall side by the door, but out of sight. The prize for winning was a streamed corn bread. If you lost the game you could eat two big bites and then you had to give away the rest to the winner. Of course, the best game of all was outsmarting the guards in any way that we could.

Sometimes we also did foolish stupid things that matched our daily lives. One time we let a man eat ten bowls of maize gruel. We decided that if he could eat all of it, it would be his for free. He sat on the stool so he could defecate while eating. He was so bloated from overeating that at last he could not do it and one bowl of maize gruel remained that he absolutely could not eat.

No cigarettes and no matches were allowed, but we found ways to smoke. When there was a prisoner being taken out for interrogation, he could ask for a time to urinate and then pick up cigarette butts from the W.C. area where the guards had discarded them. Or if a prisoner saw a cigarette butt near by, he would pretend to tie has shoelaces in order to pick up the cigarette butt from the ground. Often the interrogator might know this was happening, but generally speaking he did not care or try to prevent it. After all they were used and discarded butts. When the prisoner returned to the prison room, he could use cotton, which was in a quilt to start a fire. The only bad thing was that usually it needed to be new cotton that was without much human sweat. The cotton had to be twisted tightly and rubbed against a brick on the ground with great exertion. If the cotton was dry and became hot, it had to be quickly ripped open so you could blow on it. Sometimes if the cotton was really dry it became hot enough from the friction and would catch on fire easily.

There was a young male prisoner who I liked very much. His "crime" was from when he was a student in grade two of junior middle school. He and two other schoolmates supposedly took an oath before Jiang Jie Shi who was a deceased president of the Republic of China. Because of this he was cast into prison. His schoolmates were kept in different prison rooms. But they always took advantage of "let in fresh air" time to ingeniously keep in touch with each other. The "let in fresh air" for every room was not at the same time. He was intelligent and nimble, and when returning after the "let in fresh air" time, he always ran ahead in order to grab a little extra food without the others knowing.

I especially needed to thank him for his consideration of me. He stitched underwear for me. He was the one who not long after I arrived became ill, and then soon I was ill. By the time I recovered, it was near early summer. I was only dressed in cotton trousers, and no longer had underwear. In the summer, cotton trousers would be too hot and could not be worn with comfort. He unexpectedly stitched underwear for me using a pillow towel that he had stolen. He drew a thread from the pillow towel, and using a hook and eye from the collar on a Chinese tunic suit, he bent it into a needle. He some how used a sharp broken bowl piece as a scissors for cutting. His completed work let me avoid suffering during the summer heat. (I still have this underwear preserved today.)

With the coming of summer the prison was full of bed bugs and lice. Many prisoners were becoming ill. Soon every cell had to be fumigated with medicine. We were striped stark naked and transferred to another empty prison room. All clothes were put together and the whole room was sprayed with medicine. We were shifted across the courtyard where there were many additional prison rooms. At that time, although I thought I was recovered, I sometimes felt in a daze all day long. I often lay down on the bed and sometimes lost consciousness. One time when I was unconsciousness I felt this boy trimming my fingernails with a broken piece of bowl. Although the room was sprayed with medicine, the bedbugs and lice still did not decrease in number. Every night we were bitten by them as we dropped off asleep. Formerly, I did not know why there was only a little area of the body having bed bug bites, and then I learned. Every night when the bedbugs sucked the prisoner's blood they took a bite and then revolved a round and returned to the same place to take another bite. Therefore bedbugs bite people always in a small space. If you move, it runs away immediately. Every night I always lay for ½ hour before falling to sleep and thousands of bedbugs were suddenly stamped out in our country. Somehow it made me feel better and of some useful purpose after a useless day.

Chapter Fourteen:

Unbearable Heat

The second month of summer passed and the weather was getting hotter and hotter day by day. The prison room was filled with prisoners like we were in a food steamer. We made fans with any piece of paper, but they all were confiscated. "Let them be steamed," were the words of the administrators. On such a hot day a towel squeezed in a mug gave off a mildew smell. One day at "let in the fresh air" time, we saw many little stalks on the ground. Everyone took some and inserted them, like matchsticks, in the wall cracks and could then hang a towel. The "bad administrator" discovered it and all the towels were confiscated. One week passed and still the towels were not returned to us. But soon it was time for a "good administrator". At "let in the fresh air." time we saw him and implored him to return the towels. The next day all the towels were returned. Can you imagine not having towels to wipe off some of the sweat during the summer heat?

Owing to the severe man-made conditions of our existence, prisoners began dying. In the next room two prisoners died on the same day. One man was of the Hui nationality. Our man who climbed the window and stole a glance said that the dead man had a white cloth wrapped around his body and the guards finally carried him away. The man who was sleeping in the same bag said that in the morning when we got up and he noticed that the dead man did not move, he gave him a push, but there was no reaction.

In the summer another great pain to be suffered was thirst. Prison authorities did not give us more water due to the summer heat. We were given one ladle when thirsty. Sometimes we could not eat green soup, even if we were very hungry because it was too salty. Once a young man was too hungry so he drank more soup. At night he groaned and groaned with thirst.

In order to avoid more deaths prison authorities decided to add an additional "let in the fresh air" at night around 8PM. Two cauldrons were set in the skylight, filled with water. We were allowed the good fortune of washing. The first time we all made a run towards the cauldrons. The first prisoner put his face all the way in the water and began drinking with all his might. An administrator saw it and beat his back with a lock. He was beaten ferociously and ruthlessly, but he paid no attention to the beating until he drank enough and went back to his room. The administrator was in hot pursuit and continued to hit his back for some time in the room. I felt so devastated watching this because it was like we were oxen or horses with no human dignity.

I had recovered from my illness, but I was still very weak. It was a stipulation that during the day we must sit bolt upright on the bed. But I was unable to sit upright. There was no choice, but for me to lie on the floor. The other prisoners did not ask me to take food duty because I think that they feared I might break a bowl or spill a bucket.

During the three months that I had been in prison I had been brought to trial once. The interrogator was a young man about 30 years of age. He was fair and clear, gentile and suave. He went after me out of the public security branch bureau, which was across the street opposite the court. Originally it was the busiest section of town. The street became very familiar to me. At this hearing he ordered me to sit down and inquired about the record of my formal schooling, and the history of my work, in great detail, and at last he asked if I had anything else to say. I told him that I had much to say, but I do not remember now how much I said to him.

He asked me whether I had said, "Hong Kong engineers work at a wage of 500 Hong Kong yuan a month?" That would imply that I longed for a bourgeois life and intended to go over to the enemy. I said, "yes." I actually said "affirmative" because it is more polite. This was the first interrogation since October.

Chapter Fifteen:

A Trial—Again

I was brought to trial again at this time. The vice law district court leader Comrade Wang was present. The interrogator asked me which people I had frequent contact with. I replied strictly according to the facts that there were five natives of Shanghai. When asked what we talked about I said that I do not remember. The vice leader Wang chipped in that we were a counter-revolutionary group. I replied that you must give me the definition of a count-revolutionary group so that I can judge whether or not it applies.

"Stand up," Wang shouted in a stern voice. Then he said, "You, five or six men drank and had dinner at a restaurant. You sat here. Who sat there and there? Can you deny it?"

I laughed in my heart of hearts and thought, yes, even if you are right that we ate and drank together, how could that make us a counter-revolutionary group? I said, "We were acquaintances trying to have a good time together. Who could consider such a simple social group to be counter-revolutionary?" Wang had nothing to say in reply. The interrogator politely ordered me to sit down.

These were my only two official interrogations in my prison life of over two years. If only what took place at these interrogations were what was held against me I would not worry. There was no secrecy in my heart. We had done NOTHING wrong. But, that was as long as my friends were not forced to say something against me. With just this they could not execute me, but with false information I probably could be sentenced to death.

My pattern of social life continued at Xian Metallurgical Machine Works where I also had some close friends all from Shanghai. On Sundays or at festivals we often gathered together to do the cooking and drinking. In that painful life this was our sole time of rejoicing. We came from Shanghai, which was the target of Capitol Construction Secretary Guo. They kept watch on us all day long. There were mostly bricklayers and a good friend who had transferred to Xian Grain Distribution Station. In order to keep clear of being watched we always went to the grain distribution station to get together and have a dinner party. It definitely was the counter-revolutionary group the Vice leader Wang pointed out and we thought it was just a dinner party. Guo collected our statements of the actions and words of the day.

Later he had me engage in the hardest punishment in the "great Cultural Revolution." He put up my dazibao. He criticized and denounced me. He hung out my shingle, had my head shaved, paraded me through the streets to expose me before the public and had me locked up. Everyone who had any dealings with me was under suspicion. Even another secretary of a former capital construction group was said to have "harbored" me. He hoped to isolate me, but not one of my friends abandoned me and told lies about me.

Sometimes when we had the chance we would get together to unburden our grievances and thoughts. I had made many unwise comments. I clearly remembered that at least once I had declared Mao ZeDong as the biggest landlord in the world possessing more than 960 km2. He also was the biggest slaveholder, controlling 800,000,000 slaves. He also was one of the biggest Capitalists in the world, possessing and controlling millions and millions of dollars in wealth. He was also the biggest party chieftain of the forces of darkness.

I often lay on the floor-bed thinking of my many secret comments. Would someone betray me? They wouldn't and they couldn't, because they each knew that to do so would allow for my execution. If the Communist Party knew of the way I described our great and perfect Mao, I would be shot. At least until the last interrogation, they had not discovered my secret.

Chapter Sixteen:

A Different Prison in 1970

In November of 1970, one night all prisoners were suddenly being moved. We carried packages with our few belongings. Two men were handcuffed together. We were filed into many trucks. This was my first time being handcuffed; and it could, indeed, bring much pain to your hands and wrists. In not too long of a time we arrived at a big prison.

It was a municipal prison and had many many courtyards. It was clean and peaceful. Every courtyard had five to six prison rooms. Every prison room was about 20 square-meters. We originally had 20 prisoners in one room, but now we are divided into two groups of ten prisoners to a room. Sleeping conditions were greatly improved. "Let in fresh air" time was also wonderfully extended. We no longer had to run out in a nervous state. We could defecate in a lavatory. No man kept a constant look over us. Also no one had limited water to wash with. One day, although the weather was cold, I still ladled half a washbasin of water to scrub my body because it felt so civilized to do.

So it seemed that we had escaped from death, which was a real possibility in our previously adverse living conditions. I had been in a prison of the district public security bureau for 9 months, but the impression was that was in comparison to being in this municipal prison for 17 months. In the municipal prison I did suffer from hunger and also got very cold. But in general, our frame of mind would take a turn for the better.

This new place was opposite in many ways to the district bureau prison, where we had been. There green soup was very very salty and here there was no green soup at all. So we did not get any salt. In the municipal prison we ate salt only three times, on the two spring festivals and one national day. To my great surprise we had pork braised in brown sauce and everybody got 250 grams. The pork braised in brown sauce was salty.

Chapter Seventeen:

Work is an
Improvement in 1971

Over this period of time things seemed to be getting better in China and there was a need for a labor force. Prison authorities saw a strong labor force in the prisoners, which unfortunately, is still the case today. I worried that this did not include me because I was among the weakest of the prisoners.

It seemed that all the prisoners were content to go anywhere and do anything rather than just sit. They also could get two steamed breads instead of just one, if they started to labor. Prisoners started to compare what we were promised to the external world, which we heard about from a new prisoner. For two steamed breads you could work as a coolie. They seemed willing to face cruel exploitation rather than just sit. A future of labor seemed better than the present boring idleness.

In April of 1971, prisoners began to work. And what was our purposeful mission? A vast amount of used military uniforms were collected from the whole country and delivered to every room of our prison. We took each apart piece by piece. This was our work. We could work only six hours a day but we had to complete fixed quotas. They delivered scissors for us to use and now it was convenient to finally cut our fingernails. At this time I was still very weak and I could not even sit up for a long time. I was so thin that my backbones could be seen, one by one. I weighed only 40 kg on a balance scale. During my illness I had lost over 28 kg. So, I could not keep up with others in taking a part the uniforms. Moreover I often cut my fingers. I had developed a skin disease and my resistance was very low. Where my skin was cut or worn raw, it became infected and inflamed and would not heal. I had much pain and I would toss and turn in bed with many sleepless nights. But, I had to keep trying.

Prisoners were so willing to do any kind of labor because it was better than staying in our jail room and stupidly sitting there at attention doing nothing. To do work of any kind would give us pleasure in many ways. We especially loved collecting a few of the better buttons from the uniforms, which we kept as valuable possessions and to use in various games that we could play. During our lives as prisoners we were allowed absolutely no material wealth. But now we had "property"—buttons and material scraps that we took and hid from the guards. Of course, these possessions were not outwardly permitted, but just having the opportunity to "own" something was too great to pass up. Suddenly these poor items took on great value and losing whatever we had could be very threatening. The days in jail, I found, under the state of extreme lack of material conditions or prerequisites. People could become very stingy and possessive. Prison rules stipulated that on every holiday such as Spring Festival, New Year's Day, May 1, October 1, the guards must ransack all prison rooms. All prisoners had to leave their rooms. Every spot in the room was searched from cracks in the bed to cracks in corners. They carried out a huge search. Prisoners did everything to hide their treasured buttons. If they succeeded in escaping this disaster, they were very happy and felt lucky and rich. Originally, we had to remain in the prison rooms all day and night, but now we could come and go frequently to another area where we "worked." Life seemed better except for one big thing.

Uncertainty is the most difficult situation to handle. On a daily basis I would ask myself the following questions: Would I be allowed to live that day or would this be my last and I would be executed? Would it be by shooting or maybe something else would happen? Would I go back to the worse prison or might I go to a work farm? Would I ever be able to go to work somewhere and use my education? The people in power cannot agree on what should happen to me. Maybe I could just leave? But, where could I go? One prisoner said I should go to his near-by village to become a peasant. I thought that was a good idea—of course, much better than death.

The Communist Party asked a prisoner to straighten his clothes, sit up properly and remold his ideology. But, this was my thinking all day of my family. I remembered the past. I went over in my memory so many details of my child-hood, and times with my brothers and sisters as we grew up. My heart ached over the past, my stomach hurt in the present because it was almost always empty and my body was racked with pain from the cold. I feared the worst for the future, because I did not even know how long the future would be. These thoughts did me little good to "remold my ideology." If only there had been a book, a profes-sional book that I might have studied and researched. It would have diverted my thoughts from depression and I would not have wasted these two years of total inactivity in prison. Sorrowfully these two years of precious time of my valuable life slipped by with nothing good to show for it except that I had survived and was still alive.

Starting in September of 1971 we found that no new men were coming to prison. We all felt puzzled until November when a new prisoner arrived. We asked what he had done. He said that he was sent here just for criticizing Lin and Chen. Who is Lin? We were told that he had been the defense minister who was trying to usurp Mao's position. Who is Chen? He was Chen Boda who was a close supporter of Lin. These men held positions of power until Mao and Zhou Enlai, in a constant state of paranoia, launched a campaign against them. We didn't know particulars at the time, but history tells of the constant jockeying in the Chinese Communist Party. Oh, we can't believe that Lin is our Vice-Com-mander, Mao's close comrade-in-arms, and successor of our party. It is imbued with a most mocking thing that Lin's son had a plot to kill Mao and when Mao found out, Lin's plane "accidentally" crashed in Mongolia. Things were bad all over the Communist world.

Chapter Eighteen:

Officially Sentenced in 1972

On May 11, 1972, I was suddenly called out of my prison room and I was taken to a little room in a distant part of the building. An interrogator and another man were inside. After we all stood up at attention, they pronounced a sentence for me as an active counterrevolutionary and my punishment was to do penal labor under surveillance by the masses. The official accusations were stated as being: 1. I cried out grievances about Liu Shao Qi who was a chairman of our country. 2. I spread the power of the atom bomb. 3. I reversed (disagreed with) the verdict for an evildoer.

The interrogator told me in a passing remark that my case had actually been tried before December 1970. He said that we gave notice to your work unit to send for you and take you back, but your work unit took no notice of our decision. Recently we said that if they do not send for you and you do not go back to your work unit, we would release you. Then they sent us the cotton-padded cloth that you had asked for. We informed them again of our decision, but they still did not send for you.

I was surprised and puzzled by my sentence. There were so many of my anti-party, anti-socialism opinions on public record that I had expressed, and they had only charged me with those three uncomplicated facts. Those three facts were considered crimes to be the basis of the sentence for me to be in prison indefinitely and do penal labor. I was perplexed. I firmly believed that the interrogator had spared and protected me because if he had wanted to, he easily could have had me put to death. There was no lack of words from my own mouth to keep me from being executed. I know that the three above-mentioned crimes made the doer according to the Communist Government into a monster and demon, but one that could still go on breathing. After working several hours I was still in a state of disbelief and so I talked with another rightist and he too was amazed at how easily I had gotten off with my life.

So here I want to explain to the readers what these charges really mean. You must accept that all human beings have the same kind of heart and mind. In order to continue to live, at the moment, when our fate hangs in the balance, we all might betray another person who we care about and respect and not hesitate to forsake our conscience and what we know is right. You too could become so weak and terrible, out of the human instinct to preserve your life.

The rightist label, generally speaking, proceeds from justice and is rightly deserved. Many rightists actually had ulterior motives and spoke with malice and contempt, as I did. But, another group truly did not speak any thing and were accused for other reasons. It could have been due to their high income, for instance, my brother's father-in-law, formerly was a capitalist having a pharmaceutical factory in Shanghai. After "joint-state-private ownership" which was the principle form of state capitalism adopted during the socialist transformation of capitalist enterprises in China, his wage was over three hundred yuan a month. The wage was in fact quite high, but not as much as the CEO's in America make. But, give him a rightist label and then his wage will be cut down. After being so labeled, his wage was lowered to 72 yuan a month. The last kind of rightist label served as a stopgap for Communist quotas. The rightist quota was targeted at 10/100 in the intellectual population. Each area or work unit must attain the targets set in the state plan. So, a few of the rightists were labeled just to meet the quota of having enough rightists. Those unfortunate individuals may not have done anything, but cause a minor irritation to someone in power. Someone wrote a clever dramatic play mirroring this state of affairs, but of course, the performance was forbidden in 1980, although word of it traveled throughout the intellectual communities and we took joy in the intellectual accomplishment.

Yes, we monsters and demons worked together when we, early on, realized that the Chinese Communist Party was not what it first appeared to be, while the rest of the country went on talking and laughing as if nothing bad was happening. At that time, because I didn't learn the lesson of blind obedience, I was first called a die-hard element. They tried to make an example of me in the hopes of keeping others under control. I, never the less, would spread my view to put great men to shame and expose their hypocrisy whenever possible. This was the basis for my first charge of crying out grievances. An example and something not specifically stated was Chairman Mao's Three Great Red Banners which brought a return of three years of catastrophe. Thousands and thousands of people died of hunger due to his ignorance and power. He later gave an excuse that he had stayed in bed while others made these decisions and Mao, to his death, refused to shoulder responsibilities for his many and grave mistakes that had horrible consequences for the Chinese people.

My charges were directly related to my comments about how Chairman Liu Shao Qi got up and instituted "more enterprises with sole responsibility for their own profit or loss and fixing output quotas on a household basis." This was to remedy our country.

I had openly made the crudest comments that Mao had diarrhea everywhere. You may not know, as most Chinese do, that Mao was publicly known to have constant constipation, sometimes only having one bowel movement in a week. When a man tries so hard to live as a god, it is easy for those around him to dwell on the less flattering aspects of his being human. I also said that Liu shaved his buttocks for him and finally took the blame, another victim of Mao. It is said that Liu did very many bad things himself, besides taking the blame for mistakes Mao had made. I cannot bring myself to complain about injustice for Liu Shao Qi compared to the many injustices he dealt the Chinese people.

My explanation of the second charge of spreading the power of the atom bomb goes back to 1969 when relations between the China and USSR were strained. The country feared an attack by the USSR with nuclear weapons. In China, the people dug air-raid shelters everywhere. On our streets, at schools, post offices, hospitals and bulletin boards everywhere possible, it was publicized how to build and survive the atomic bomb in a shelter. All of the talk at our Company was about the significance that we were at a distance of 10km from the city-center which we assumed would be the target of an atomic bomb. All the people wondered that if the belfry would be dropped at the center of the city, how would things be here for us? I had strongly stated that we could not evade disaster at that distance. Probably nowhere could a person be sparred the consequences of nuclear fall-out. Most people could not comprehend the power of a nuclear bomb. I had a better idea than most people and my desire to educate my co-workers likely was the reason for the accusation of my spreading atomic terror.

As to my third charge of disagreeing with the verdict of an evildoer, this obviously pointed towards my friend, the bricklayer to whom I had complained of unfairness. What guilt of crimes should he have? With Mao's socialism and the Chinese era of party politics and law—the country had "three-in-one" public security which also could be three-in-one absolute terror for some people. If you had an estrangement with your political leader then you could be given a hard time for the rest of your life. One political leader could be your administrative officer (supervisor or boss), your public prosecutor, your police officer as well as your judge. That was too much power to have in the hands of one man. Your administrative leader could catch hold of your words only one time and confront you with the possibility of death. We all have experienced the difficulty of a "bad boss" at work, but then it became our system in China for him to hold the power of life or death over our heads. That is a terror which everyone can understand.

The secretary of the construction section, Guo, in this respect left himself no avenue of retreat. Obviously to pronounce me guilty was Guo's expectation. That day I was moved to another room, which held only two other men who were intellectuals also. They had been sent to prison owing to "veiled criticism" against our Vice commander, Mao's successor Lin Biao. But after Lin Biao was cast out of government after eight months, they should have been set free. This was the situation for me to disagree with the verdict of an evil doer.

On May 12, 1972, in the afternoon, a truck of metallurgical machine workers came to the prison. That same truck would be used to take me away. When it was time for the truck to leave, I saw that my simple baggage was put on the back and then I had to see an office secretary named Comrade Wang Shu Ji, my savior. It was he who was getting me out of the prison. He was a new arrival on the staff. He was a Communist too, but he strove to do things properly and humanely for me and other lucky ones.

As I climbed up into the truck, I looked around. From this time on I would leave this most barbarous place forever and ever. It was a place of human famine and unbelievable human crowding causing much illness and death. It was a place of not enough water and either no salt needed by the body or excessive salt. It was a place of no medicine, no padded clothing in the cold and one towel with cotton wadding and one small cup for water when it was hot. For two years I had had no bath and I had not brushed my teeth. **This was a place of remolding one's ideology in name, but cruel tyranny in reality.** Its sins were too great in number for me to mention further, but they cannot get erased from my mind and fill me with grief and anger to this day.

CHAPTER NINETEEN:

TIME ON A WORK-FARM IN 1972

On the truck I broke down in tears because I was so overwhelmed with relief and I had not eaten in so long. I realized that I was beyond hunger. I needed food soon or I would die of lack of energy to breathe.

After a relatively short drive, the truck stopped at a farm that belonged to our Company in San Yuan County, 50 km from Xian. This was an area of saline-alkali soil. Water was pumped from a well and irrigated saline-alkali soil in order to grow rice. But what I remember the most is what a dinner I had that night! I had enough to eat. Also I obtained a healthy amount of salt. It had been one year since I knew the taste of salt. The head farmer saw that I was eating so fast and perhaps too much. He was afraid that I would burst my stomach, so he informed the cook to limit my quantity. But whenever I could, I went to a little shop near the farm to buy more food in secret.

At the work farm I was able to see the life of the poor and lower-middle peasants of this locality. Their lives, the little food they ate and their shabby apparel made me feel sad and my eyes filled with tears. I felt that as long as the Communist Party did nothing, the Chinese people could live well. Oh my God, I prayed please let them do nothing more often!

I hadn't thought much of the plight of the farmers and peasants, but now I remembered in 1962, that Mao Zedong had made a speech at the seven thousand people's plenary session. He said," Our peasant's hearts are so kind, they would rather die in a famine than ever rise up in a rebellion." Today the famine has passed away and many of them did die, but others lived and have had perhaps worse, a terrible existence. But, he had forgotten what our peasants had provided and so he punished them again.

In the early 1960's political movements were coming back. At first, it was required learning about Lei Feng who was a soldier-peasant killed in 1962 after leaving an "inspirational" diary about unswerving devotion to the Maoist cause. Then came the cruel "four cleanups movement." Shortly after people started being able to eat their fill, the movements also started to create other misery in our lives. In 1964 to1965 the "four clean ups movement" pressed us harder and harder. It was a fresh campaign against "right revisionists." We held political meetings every night. The high-level work team was accountable for every action. There was emphasis on the value of "class struggle." This movement was mostly aimed at the countryside, but in the city, all areas of work also became very stern. The pattern was to identify "ideological enemies" and then criticize and denounce, hit and make them kneel. They needed to be "cleaned-up" in what-ever way possible.

Another "land reform" was issued. Many families were replenished as land-lords or rich peasants, but also many families were swept out of the door. At my company, many workers were punished too. A bricklayer, my close friend who was in the same workshop said that our secretary was "a sheep's head who sells dog meat." He was punished as an "evildoer" then an incantation of the golden hoop was tied on his head. His whole life would come to an end because of the "four clean ups movement." Fatiguing interrogations continued all day and all night and cruel beatings impelled our company. One man, the store man, was hanged by the neck.

Another man, a worker in the mess hall, jumped from a high place, but instead of dying, he experienced the continuing horror of being a cripple. He admitted that he had stolen one sack of wheat flour during the famine. When criticized he was accused of stealing 5 sacks of flour. But he adamantly would not admit to having stolen 5 sacks. Regardless what the pressure, he would not admit. They would not let him sleep and they hit him until he was covered with bruises and injuries. What could be the basis of accusing him of having stolen five sacks of flour instead of one? The work team investigated his family members. They asked his wife and she said "one sack." They asked his father who also said, "one sack." They asked his son and daughter, who both said, "one sack." He had admitted stealing one sack and so instead of considering that they were all referring to the same sack, it became a more serious accusation of stealing five sacks, which he would not admit to, because it was not true. The "four clean ups movement" soon undermined the very people who had survived and recovered from the famine.

Unfortunately, my new location allowed me to have new insights into the horrors of the Chinese Communist Party in a new way, of how the farmers and peasants were treated. Previously I had experienced what the CCP did to intellectuals and highly talented and competent Chinese workers. I had never focused my awareness on the plight of the Communist farmer like I was able to now.

CHAPTER TWENTY:

SICK BODY, CURED SPIRIT

Secretary Wang told the farm leader to let me do light physical labor. The second day there the farm leader asked me to sweep the courtyard. As I swept my legs felt heavier and heavier. The third day I thought that I had developed dropsy. A doctor who was also a laborer at the farm looked at me. He seemed like an old friend. He told me to not use so much salt and I knew that, but I could not resist. The fourth day my legs swelled and my skin started cracking. Of course, it gave me much pain and I could hardly walk.

I was given permission to ride a bicycle to the San Yuan County Hospital which was10 km from the farm to see a doctor. Just as I had gone two kilometers my bicycle broke down. Fortunately, there was a town where I could repair it. During the repair, the worker accidentally noticed that my legs were so swollen. He asked me about it and then said that I need not travel to the county hospital because this town also had a hospital with a famous doctor of traditional Chinese medicine named Feng, who the government had forced to work in this little town.

When I got to the hospital in the little town, I saw that many patients were lined up to see the famous Chinese medicine doctor. There was no one to see the doctor of western medicine. I was afraid to be the only one to see the Doctor of Western Medicine, but I was in too much pain to be able to wait. The Western doctor looked and felt my legs and seemed puzzled. He then consulted with the Chinese Medicine Doctor holding a group consultation of all the doctors practicing both Chinese and Western medicine. They all seemed perplexed, but decided to give me a tonic and a coupon for one kg. of brown sugar. Oh, how precious—sugar, it had been years since I had that taste.

Several days later I went to another hospital because I was not getting better. A young woman doctor trained in Western medicine said that it could be one of three problems. She said that dropsy can have three causes. One problem could be that my heart has a disease. The second problem could be that my kidneys have a disease. The third cause could be severe malnutrition. She thought that it had to be problems one or two because for some reason she thought that I was an official of the town. She could not understand how I could be experiencing malnutrition. She did not even consider the possibility of my having been a prisoner and she did not ask me about my living conditions. She gave me another tonic and royal jelly. I smiled in my heart and knew that the kindhearted doctor had completely cured me because she made me feel of human value. I was mistaken for an official. I was no longer "nothing" from a prison. I would survive because I now was a valuable human being with dignity.

Within two months I put on 30 kilograms and attained the weight of 70 kg. My neck became thick and grew faster than the two pigs that I was raising. My pigs did not want to grow up, but they soon could run faster than dogs. I also had a little black pet dog that became my constant companion and friend. The dog also offered me dignity and love. I learned that **human worth ranks with oxygen, water and food as a necessity** to keep one alive.

After I arrived at the farm, I first wrote to ask about my brother in Shanghai and his marriage. God had blessed him with a good baby daughter, now one-year-old. Upon hearing this wonderful news the stone in my heavy heart dissipated giving me a new joy and lightness like I had forgotten existed.

Meanwhile I received a parcel post box with two suits of cotton jersey and trousers. Oh, how much I needed that. My older sister seemed to know just what I needed. Thinking of my family members made me determined to stay alive and become healthy. They knew that I was in such bad health having dropsy. My third sister wanted to come to the farm to see me, but it was not allowed. The reason given was that I was still in a state of ideological remolding and she might arrest my progress. It is significant that just to the contrary, what could have helped me most was the inspiration of my family. The Communist Party, at that time just as now too, I deemed as having a venomous heart and a small mind. They simply do not understand the true nature of humanity. We are social creatures and the strongest ties are within the nuclear and extended family. The government cannot take the place of familial love and the emotional connections of shared experiences and struggles on an intimate level. Communism simply does not consider human nature. It can't work in the long run because it goes against our very humanity.

They also do not understand man's need for justice. One should receive, as he deserves. The harder and smarter you work the more benefits you should receive from your labor. If a man has to share everything that he has earned, he loses motivation for work. The only ones who are happy getting equal to what everyone else gets, are those who have worked less than others. With a system like that, soon no one wants to work. Even the men at the prison worked harder and longer not out of duty, but in the hope of discovering and keeping the best buttons, which were personally earned rewards.

I passed through a time when I learned more about human nature. I discovered that our farmers, who all came from our Xian Metallurgical Machine Works Company, were arrogant toward the local peasants. They considered that compared with the peasants they were in an advantageous position of having more education and training and coming from other locations. Maybe the peasants were too poor and they envied the worker's wages, although it all was terribly little that everyone received. The peasants never have money, but they can barter and trade their daily salt in exchange for eggs or produce. At the end of the year, if there is something left after the crop is sold, they may get a share of a little money to spend as they desired.

Our company farm had sunk a well and drew water every day. It made the peasants wells go dry. So the peasants had to walk to our well and carry water in containers on their shoulders from our farm. But, the workers did not want to allow the peasants to draw the water once our pump was in operation. They wanted to hoard the water for our own use and not share with the other farmers. I communicated with every farmer's family when they came to draw the water and carry it. I began to get in touch with the farmers. They are mostly good and honest. I was amazed to find out why they were so poor. San Yuan County is mostly a rich area, which abounded in cotton and rice. But the farmers were still badly off. They lived in houses made of dirt, ate maize gruel with a little added chili powder and wore worn out clothes. The children's facial expressions were dull-witted, especially in the winter. I saw that the children usually wore old and shabby black jackets that were so thin you could see through the cotton padding. They wore no underwear. In one hand they carried a big bowl and looked at me with a dull light in their eyes. This started to make my heart worried for China's future.

These people lead a true Communist life. Every team ate the same food. Maize was the main harvest. They all ate maize. Sweet potatoes were all dug together and then everyone ate sweet potatoes. Chilies were grown and picked together and then they all ate chilies. Vegetable greens were picked and they all ate vegetable greens. Of course, they only ate the produce that was not fit to send to the city. They all had little bowls, like little washbowls. There was no money all year except at the end of the year. At this time they got money from the production brigade. In previous times they could go to the cooperative shop taking eggs to exchange for salt, noodles or other things. But now eggs were very few because raising a large number of hens was no longer allowed. Mao had ruled against that. When children came from school they cut grass for the pigs and put the ewe out to pasture. The children did have a great quantity of milk to drink. It was a very simple and hard life.

I heartily sympathized with the farmers. I felt like I had become a farmer's good friend. Also they had not discriminated against me on account of my being called a rightist. Their team was allowed to slaughter one or two pigs for the Spring Festival and share it with all the farmer's families. At Spring Festival they ate steamed buns stuffed with pork. But it is only two times that farmers got to eat pork. I remember that when in the municipal prison, I also had two times to eat meat, although the total amount was less than 50 grams.

On Spring Festival Eve, the farmers invited me to eat minced meat in steamed stuffed buns. The first day of Spring Festival the team leader invited me to eat noodles and meat. I was their only guest. For more than one year while I was there at the farm I developed a deep affection for farmers. My farm leader felt that I was taking things too seriously. He questioned me because I was supposed to be a rightist and counterrevolutionary. Then, why did I care so much for others and the farmers welcome me to be with them?

Chapter Twenty-One:

Back to the Work Unit
in 1973

In September of 1973, without explanation or warning, I received orders to go back to my work unit.

Before parting I said good-bye to the farmers since this was a very uncertain journey and I did not know if I would ever see them again. We all wept and I especially cried bitterly because I had found that I never deviated in my character and heart from my good and honest farmer-brothers. The truck was waiting for me. The farmer-brothers gave me steamed bread, sweet potatoes, pomegranates and some gave me raw eggs. But it was decided at the last minute that I could not travel on such a long trip with raw eggs without breaking them. So the truck had to wait longer while the eggs were boiled. The Farm Leader got angry that this "rightist" was so cared for by the farmers. He felt that the farmers should pay closer attention to others' political points of view.

On returning to my work unit I was assigned the job of being a grit cleaner which means that I used a pneumatic shovel to remove grit from big castings. So it was considered that in the steel-casting workshop, I did "penal labor under surveillance by the masses."

My first night back at the company, I was put in the guesthouse. My friends secretly came to see me and each narrated his hard luck of the past years. They also told me of the great efforts that were taken in order to uncover the facts of our "counterrevolutionary group." I was told that each of my friends was locked up apart from the others.

The official story went that one man among us had his family threatened. He was unable to bear up under the threats and afflictions so he confessed that I was the commander and he was the minister of foreign affairs and others held various positions. But, he never had any evidence for his accusations because obviously there couldn't be any for the stories that he had fabricated while under duress.

I thought into the night about all the things I had been told that evening. I remembered that this man who betrayed us was a native of Shanghai and really wasn't very close with any of us. When we were ferreted out he was as proud as a peacock to be with us and he never seemed cold and indifferent. One day he was ferreted out and then became closer to us. He built ties of friendship and had a closer hand in our lives. But it turned out it was only to spy on us. As soon as he exposed us and he thought he had rendered a service, he never showed interest in us again. It seemed like he was almost planted as a spy or quickly took that position when threatened.

I could not believe that our having an active counterrevolutionary group was tenable to anyone. Consequently in our company everybody was talking about this matter. Actually the organization of the Communist Party knew that it all was an out-and-out fabrication. They were accustomed to embellished reports, which they often required of people. They did this to play with us and to see how much pressure a person could stand. But, I was concerned that they had heard of another matter and might pay attention to it. Someone had also said that I had wanted to go over to the enemy. And this really had happened.

A short time after I arrived in Xian, I had mentioned to a few others that I had been thinking about the possibility of hiding in a cave in Changan County, which was 20 km from Xian. At the time, we had all been expecting a war with Russia. My idea was that when USSR would storm into China, I would go to their side. I knew enough Russian and that my engineering background would be valuable to an invading army and new military government. Apparently the man from Shanghai had produced a photograph, which showed a bed, and a military can in it. The proclaimed photograph was a counterfeit. I had never been to the caves, but just had heard of them and that others were thinking of going there. I had been a close friend of an apprentice from Changan, who worked on the same scaffold team. In 1969 relations between China and USSR were strained. In

1970, our government started to move criminals that had been relocated to Qinghai back to the east. I was certain that once USSR invaded China, they would be sure to kill the "5 kinds of elements" that were being held in Laogai because they knew we would defect. I made up my mind to escape from Xian one step ahead. This apprentice knew there were caves in Changan. He was willing to help me to succeed in escaping this catastrophe, to tell me where I might hide myself and he even got things prepared for me. As for this military can, it was borrowed from me easily. This matter was ferreted out as front-page news. Before I returned to my company, I was absolutely ignorant that these ideas had been exposed.

Now there were the "four kinds "of people, at this time, that Mao said that he wanted, which were landlords, slaveholders, capitalists and party chieftains of the forces of darkness. Why I was not exposed with the facts about my numerous crimes I will never know. This would have caused me to be put to death. Originally they took the same action or view without prior consultation, attributing all this to being a traitor. Because of this, it allowed me to escape a deadly blow and maintain my miserable life, instead.

I realized long after I was released from prison that I was spared because of my wage. It happened at the meeting of the community-court. The new secretary, Wang had vowed to counteract as much as possible what the former secretary of the capital construction section, now the director of political department, Gou had done. He had proposed omitting my wage and substituted living expenses. Wang firmly believed this would be harmful, keep me from remolding my ideology, and he finally would have won. There were some good persons in the party, but they found themselves having a problem which put them in a sorry plight. They would forever remain a lower officer and would not be promoted. Most of the members who advanced had a vicious hostile conviction. Some times, I have great sympathy for those Communist Party officers, even if they have done bad things, provided it is not seriously evil minded. I am willing to forgive them, because if they had done any differently, they would not be allowed to continue at their post and might also put themselves and their very lives in jeopardy.

What was wrong with the theory and purpose of Communism? Communism does not ask its members to persecute the masses. Contrarily, its hope was to build a classless society that would be an earthy paradise. But, many men misused the name of revolution to gain power and this was richly appealing to many. After gaining the power then they took Communism in their own direction. The real Communist Party member would not forget what he had said when he took the oath on being admitted to the party. He would stay true to the high ideals of Communism, but there were not many of these people.

CHAPTER TWENTY-TWO:

A REVIEW OF ROBERT'S FAMILY

I had lived a very boring life in the Laogai with too much time to think and worry. I thought mostly about my family—so many brothers and sisters who I hadn't seen or heard from in years. All I could do was to wonder how they were, were they in prison too and were they alive? At the time, I did not have any information and so all I could do was imagine what might be happening. I cannot explain how hard this was. *The unknown has to rank among the greatest of demons and one of the worst kinds of human torture.*

After all that I had worried about over my years in prison, I finally obtained the right to go home to visit my family. My leave to go home was to last twenty days. This was the first time that I had gotten out of the Laogai and was able to return to Southern China including Nanjing, Shanghai and Hangzhou. I wanted to see all my family members.

My first stop was in Nanjing to see my younger brother. I had missed him very much. He too hated the Communist party and considered it as imperious and despotic, the same as I felt. He also liked to lay bare the spirit of revolution against the Communist party. When he was in college, he found that many letters being sent to him were being opened. Early on he complained to the Communist party, angrily. He called the college authorities into account and swore that they did not have the most rudimentary legal knowledge. This situation has still not been corrected and letters, to this day, are opened by the government. Originally he had loved and esteemed the Communist Party as so many did when they first took over, but now he became in opposition to them.

We had frequently pointed out the trends of the time with government errors and offer salutary advice in our communications by letters and actually sometimes, we bitterly attacked the government. He succeeded in escaping a more severe rightist punishment because he disappeared to the countryside to do manual labor. He was eventually criticized, denounced and locked up in a cowshed, but no rightist hat was ever put on his head. He remained faithful and unyielding.

I could remember that one day in the long ago past suddenly many letters, which had been gathered together and held for a long time, were given to me at once. I noticed that the date on one of them was one month before. Some letters that had been sent by my brother were in the pile. We did not refrain from using scathing denounced words, as evidenced in these letters. The next day is when I was locked up in the basement of my company.

How could I not worry about him for his safety and the danger he could be in? He was thirty-nine years old. He too had been in love with a wonderful woman. I didn't know whether he was locked up and if his political problems had also destroyed his relationship. And then I saw him and his daughter. Oh, what a lovely baby he and his wife had!

The next day, my brother accompanied me to see their security section. He had warned them that his older brother was coming, but the security section was unable to make heads or tails of the problem. At first they thought, your brother is coming, and what way will that concern us? "Our brother was labeled a counterrevolutionary," said my other brother. The third day of my visit, the public security committee and officers from the police substation came to meet me. I do not know why they were being so neurotic. They brought a piece of paper for me to fill out. I fiddled about with it, taking my time to appear I was being through. A police officer picked it up and examined it carefully. As it turned out and we found out later, my brother lived in half of a thatched cottage beside his company. On the opposite half of the thatched cottage lived a young worker. The relationship between him and my brother was friendly, but the man was under orders to keep watch on the movements of my brother which included my visit. Afterwards he said to my brother, after he had discovered my brother was upright, that he was sorry to have to be in such a position. My brother later looked upon this neighbor as a true friend.

Next I went to Hangzhou where most of my other brothers and sisters were living. We had all passed through an unheard of calamity called "the great Cultural Revolution." Fortunately, all my family was safe, sound and thankfully alive, though most had suffered immensely and permanently. It was such a relief to make the journey, see each family member and embrace them as if we all had returned from the grave. I want to tell you many of the things that I learned had happened to various family members.

My youngest sister and her husband who met at the office where they worked had gotten divorced. Her husband had to return to his native place—Shang yu, Zhejiang Province. His work now was to carry a pole on his shoulders acting a lacquerer. My sister returned to Hangzhou to try to find some other means of livelihood. She had no registered permanent residence and therefore was given no grain coupons which made it very hard for her to live. When I could, I sent her ten yuan every month to try to save her life. Since I was locked and had no small wage to share with her, I wrote to her and I told her I couldn't send her money any more. Thinking that she had no source of income reduced me to tears. Later I found out that they did not even send the letter for me as they had said they would.

My second eldest sister had studied and worked at a missionary hospital. She made a profound friendship with a woman officer from New Zealand. In 1958, on these thin grounds of "knowing a foreign missionary" she had been sent to receive reeducation through labor. She had to leave a five-year-old son in my third sister's care. Her husband had also been sent away, owing to his past record. He was sent to a far away small village. They finally had no choice but to divorce. She concluded her reeducation through labor in 1962, and returned to Hangzhou. She then had no source of income with her son to also support. I had so much to think about.

My oldest brother had become a doctor and was a very honest and upright man. In the "Great Cultural Revolution" he also was locked up. He was compelled to tell about a certain person. My brother racked his brain and said all the names of people who he had known. But, he did not mention the name of the one they wanted him to say. The interrogation was going on day and night. He wanted to jump out of a high window, but was obstructed. At last he begged them to say who they wanted to know about. They finally gave him the name, but my brother still did not know who this person was. It turned out the young man whose name they wanted was my younger brother's schoolmate and he had borrowed an umbrella from my younger brother at Wuhan. He had forgotten to return it. But later he gave this umbrella back to my eldest brother in Shanghai at a very brief encounter. That was their only contact, ever. This schoolmate of my younger brother was later criticized and denounced at Wuhan. He confessed all the people he had known. He thought of my eldest brother's name although he had no specific memories about him. For this, can you call it, reason; my oldest brother's life was almost taken in prison. It is insane that one person "in trouble" to save himself can simply give another person's name which in turn gets that person in trouble also.

My third sister was a mid-wife. She looked after my younger sister's daughter who my younger sister could not take care of. This five-year-old niece sat in an office all day. The girl played and read treasured books with quotations from Chairman Mao. One day she was not careful, as a five-year-old can't be all of the time. She spilled a little ink on the red treasured book. Then my sister was criticized and denounced and was locked up as a reactionary. What had become of my third sister now? What about my little niece?

My oldest sister was a teacher at a primary school in Shanghai. She had been there for thirty years and didn't get married because she had to constantly support all her younger brothers and sister in Shanghai while they were studying and later to help them with the cost of living and surviving. I also had asked her for money. She always borrowed from her women colleagues. Her colleagues were willing to loan money to her because the whole school called her "eldest sister." She was a good and honest woman and was always willing to help others. Later, at the time of her retirement, her headmaster asseverated in public that, "she was a good sister, a good teacher and we all should learn from her." But, she too, during the Great Cultural Revolution was attacked with "Da Zi Bao."

Oh, my old mother, I worried about her the most. She had had eight sons and daughters and together we could not give her enough money to dress warmly and to eat as much as she needed. In China, this was the greatest shame for children.

Our great old house in Hangzhou had been invaded and occupied by the Communist Troops. Originally there lived our one family with many rooms and much space. Now ten families lived in the same home. My three sisters were still there, but they lived in three little rooms. They all had at one time married, but now they all lived alone. When the Cultural Revolution came they all were criticized and denounced. One day many Red Guards came from a near-by school and beat my younger sister. They turned over a stool and made my sister kneel over the wooden legs. They did not even spare the five-year-old daughter of my sister. They searched our house and confiscated any property. They tore our old photo albums and our genealogy tree to pieces. They plundered our calligraphies and paintings, either destroying them or taking them. They burned our memorial tablet of our ancestry and sold two exquisite shrines. They even tipped our father's bones and ashes into the trash. They pried open the floor boards and unearthed where there had been buried gold and jewelry, but it had already been taken and now nothing was found. Three of the tenants hoped that this would drive our sisters away. These tenants formerly were our friends because we had helped them. But, now they bothered and harassed my sisters everyday. It seems that they wanted them to move so they could alone occupy our home, but the sisters would not leave. I later found out that my sisters in Hangzhou experienced other tortures and torments by the Communist soldiers too numerous and terrible for me to say. It grieves me so much to have to think about it and it was so embarrassing for my sisters that it is unspeakable for me to tell you.

Since 1974, I went to visit my family every year and to see our coming generation, getting together was joyful and agonizing. My unduly punished sisters still lived in the rooms of our former home. Older nephews and nieces after graduating from junior middle school were all deprived of further education even though they were very intelligent. Instead, they had to go to the countryside and mountain areas to work. The longest time to be gone was my niece who left for nine years. This sadly exhausted all her youth and she lost all prospects for a better future. The younger children were growing poorer and had little hope for their lives to improve. What a sad result for a once prosperous, educated and hard working family. My grandfather had done nothing wrong except work hard to build a lucrative business. There was no reason for his family to suffer for his hard work and ingenuity. I do not see this as a tenant of Communist theory, but it certainly became a great part of Communist practice.

Chapter Twenty-Three:

Harassment Continues

Several days after returning to Xian, when I was working, someone from the security section called me. I thought that they might ask me to report on the situation of my going home to visit my family. When I came to the security section, a comrade Guo, who was responsible for supervising me, told me that two cadres came from Sichuan province, on the quiet. I thought that I knew at once who they were. I had two schoolmates, who in 1959, shifted their work assignment from Anshan to Chengdu. They had been very close friends. Oh, no, they must be coming to investigate something involving all of us. I was on edge, to say the least.

Two middle-aged men with strange faces in all ernestness ordered me to take a seat opposite them. They then confirmed my name and identity. They asked me in a interrogative tone, "how did you remold?" When I heard this asked by these two unexplained men, I immediately flared up in anger. I said that I think people, who are not relatives or close friends, dare not ask me such a question in such an impolite tone. After all, I am not a convict, but I am an unyielding man. I then asked them, "Where do you come from?" They said that I shouldn't bother myself about where they came from. We are asking you, how did you remold? I was so angry at their impertinence that I cried out, "What do you want?" I then said, "Don't bother yourself about my ideological remolding, if you want to interrogate me with no explanation, in that case, you will get nothing from me."

I turned my head towards comrade Guo to look at his expression. He just was smiling at me instead of frowning in disapproval. It made me deeply grateful that he seemed supportive of me. After this, their attitudes softened and they said they were coming from Sichuan, to find out what I was doing from 1953 to 1955. I then explained that I had translated a book on the automatic control of steel rolling mills from the Russian edition under the leadership of Mr. Wu. I was angry again and said that this had happened twenty years ago, and I wondered why it had not been cleared up to require their visit? At that point they replied that it was too tangled up to uneasily unravel. Again they asked, "What did you do?" I explained some more that at that time, major equipment was all made in the USSR and drawing standards and control operations were all written in Russian. If a man doesn't know Russian, how could he correctly work with the equipment? How could he know about the proper operations? For this reason, we translated this book. I then asked, "What was wrong with that? What have you hunted down and discovered? What was done twenty years ago that still disturbs you?" As for my two schoolmates in Chendu, they did not have a hand in the translation, so I concluded that this had nothing to do with them. I did not understand what they wanted to investigate? Under my stern and indignant denouncement, they went away gloomily.

I still was asking myself, what were they coming here to do? What were they actually investigating? I had hoped to be free of questioning and accusations.

Then suddenly I realized that there was an ulterior motive for this unexplained "investigation" of me and it was an excuse for them to go site-seeing on government money. Xian is an ancient capital and a wonderful place to see. I remembered that years ago others in my company and the Communist Party had used an investigation of my past as an excuse to go to Hangzhou many times. Upon returning they talked about Hangzhou's beauty and were profuse in praise of the "important trip." Finally it was unavoidable to conclude what their true purposes were and I could relax again.

Chapter Twenty-Four:

Great Upheavals in China in 1976

In January of 1976, our Premier, Zhou Enlai died, causing a great upheaval in the Communist Party. Zhou Enlai was considered to be one of the wisest and best of the Communist leaders. He was educated in Japan and France and during his time in power he maintained a world perspective for China. One of his early positions in the CCP was as director of an important military academy. This made him instrumental in both the political and military development of Chinese Communism. During the Cultural Revolution he tried to moderate Mao's policies and ideas because they often differed in both philosophy and detail. Zhou Enlai was responsible for getting first, Henry Kissinger and then President Nixon to China in 1972. He was a close friend and supporter of Deng Xiaoping who later became another positive leader of China encouraging modernization and economic liberalization.

There are always problems and drama in life and politics. First, Deng Xiaoping was held responsible for the protest at the mass memorial for Zhou. Tens of thousands of mourners were violently dispersed after they protested the influence of the Gang of Four in addition to grieving the loss of Zhou Enlai.

Also that year, Mao suffered two heart attacks, one in May and another in June. In July, in Dangshan, a northern industrial city there occurred violent earthquakes where seven hundred thousand people died as was reported by government sources, which means that it probably was a lot more. Then Mao ZeDong died on September 9, in Beijing.

Many people felt that probably "the God" must be angry with China. To others, it did not make sense. There was hope for many with the deaths of our leaders, especially when Mao died, but people wondered why "the God" would demand that so many good, honest and innocent Chinese people be buried alive in the earthquake?

Another great political force and interesting story in China was called the "Gang of Four" and it fell from power the same year, less than a month after Mao's death. Millions of people felt that they had been saved and our nation seemed to join in jubilation. This "Gang of Four" including Jiang Qing (Mao's wife), and her three closest associates abused their powers for over thirty years. Once Mao died, the others fell right away. They were placed under arrest on October 6. I never expected this "Gang of Four" to fall this way. Once their protector was gone, their own communist party wanted them not only out of power, but totally out of public contact. No one really knew what had happened to them. These four individuals, who had killed many persons and often made life worse for the entire country, apparently went scot-free and were never exposed and criticized, they just disappeared from public view. But then, finally, in 1980 to 1981 there was a "show trial" of Jiang Qing and her associates who claimed they only followed orders from Mao. They were spared execution, but remained in prison for the rest of their lives. Jiang Qing finally hanged herself.

Another important person from my past also had a bad year. I talked before of people who changed their identity to fit with whoever was in power. They also tend to rise to positions of power such as becoming chairman of the board or general manager, or perhaps in modern times, the capitalist who exploits a company and later the facts prove he was the most unscrupulous person ruining the company and lives of employees, all for personal gain. That he be found a person guilty of corruption is nothing strange, because it all starts from one idea—to be bent solely on personal profit and caring for nothing else. The man who I am referring to is capital construction section manager; Guo and he is exactly that type of character. After Mao died, he was one of the first men to go wildly corrupt. He was, at last, caught due to collusion with unscrupulous merchants. He was expelled from the party and his son was arrested as a very young man. That they both came to disgraceful ends was not an accident. I will never forget the four human lives of people I knew who were killed by him and he actually deserved worse.

CHAPTER TWENTY-FIVE:

I WILL NEVER LEARN

As I think back on Chinese History it appears to me that Chinese civilians can be the most docile people in the world and it is pitiful that they are so easy to dominate. This seems to be true from the beginning of Chinese recorded history and then became the epitome of proper behavior in the philosophy of Confucius, which had at its core the total dominance of the emperor and then males in every way. It was also true during the terror and domination of the warlords that the people lived by the whim of whoever had the most power. In more recent history it continued with the Japanese take-over, to the Guomingdang and finally now with the Chinese Communist Party. To me it seems that the Chinese people surely had more grief and domination than any other group of humans. They have endured every hardship and did little or nothing to try to stop it. My personality is so different from this that it is hard for me to understand my Chinese ancestors and brothers. Of course, I have paid dearly for my different outlook.

But at this moment, not having adequate housing was the real and pressing problem in China. In the thirty years since the supposed "liberation" of China, the housing issue had not been addressed. The population had increased by one hundred per cent, thanks to Mao's encouragement to reproduce to make China stronger. This may have worked well for the peasants who could build their own dirt houses with simple dirt room additions as needed. The big problem was for the educated people who lived in the city and like at our company had reached the age of forty and still could not marry because there was no place for a couple to live. We only had dormitory type housing with men and woman being separated. If people wanted to get married, it was impossible.

My family home in Hangzhou where we formerly lived as one family, now housed ten households. I wondered if there was no housing built, how long it would be until these most docile of people had no choice but to revolt. After the death of Mao, the government began building a great deal of housing.

I said before that regardless how severe the punishment, I did not learn to be quiet and simply take whatever injustice was being given out. I'm not sure how I got to be so different from my Chinese brothers who seemed to bare everything. They were too docile and I needed to work on that quality for myself. The most recent issue that I felt was intolerable to stay quiet about came about when our company asked workers to work extra shifts or extra hours with no pay. This happened often. Especially on Sundays in China, it was a common sight to be working with no pay. The government didn't seem to think that there was anything to our lives except to work.

But there was one step worse that I do not understand how the leaders had the impudence to enforce. There came a new rule that if you did not come in on Sunday to perform the work obligation, you would have a day's wages deducted. We didn't get paid for Sunday, so it had to be a different day's wages that was taken. This enraged me! I asked supervisors, "Which day's wages will be deducted? Monday's? Tuesday's? for not working on a day that we are not paid for?" I really was unable to hold back my indignation at such unjust hegemonies. Oh! How outrageous this seemed to me!

But no other person in my company agreed with me and wanted to fight for the most precious thing that life is made of—time. Instead, they all picked on me and said that "the counterrevolutionary has come out in the open to attack the party again." They found a young worker who did not take part in the labor obligation that Sunday and asked him to say that I had tried to persuade him not to work. I was on my way to trouble again, but he insisted that he did not come on Sunday for other reasons that had nothing to do with me. The goal of getting me in trouble again could not be attained at that time.

Next they criticized and denounced me on my team, at my work section and at my work meetings. The most interesting meeting was the workshop section meeting. That day the director of the workshop, Liu, was coming. The meeting began with a worker making a speech. I don't know what he was saying because I had more interesting things to be thinking about, but suddenly it had seemed to become a criticism of me. I had recently published an article in a foreign magazine. It told about Japan and how in developing their economy after World War II they increased production to one million tons of steel. I described what measures the government had taken and how America had improved the administration of their enterprises. Director Liu had asked me questions during the meeting but afterward he suddenly realized some error he wanted to point out. In a flash he turned his head and cried "Robert, what did you say a moment ago?" I said, "Sorry director Liu, the meeting and discussion are over." Why did he not find fault with me earlier during the meeting? Should I always be available for his comments and criticism? It was time for our midday meal. We should have a right to food, as little and tasteless that it was.

I planned on doing my normal work in the afternoon. After our mealtime my section chief came to me and said, "This afternoon we will take a meeting just to criticize and denounce you, don't be afraid." Those words were meant just the opposite that I needed to be afraid. I felt that I was a veteran of threats and punishment and I was getting immune to it all. But, this situation became a huge surprise and this section chief, it turned out, treated me with the best of intentions. It deeply moved me because I learned that many people had interest in my article from hearing the brief criticisms in the morning and truly wanted more information and so we had a good discussion under the guise of denouncing me. But, I later listened to the radio and heard that it was being reported that a counter revolutionary was provoking the young workers to sabotage obligatory labor. But they did not do anything else to me yet.

CHAPTER TWENTY-SIX:

COMMUNIST POLITICS CHANGES

Among so many comrades at my work unit, I most detested the woman director of our workshop named Shao. She was a former electric welder and served as the woman committee member on our work team. Then suddenly she became the vise-director of our company. She won promotion with such high speed that it surprised us and made us ask, how could that be? She did not do serious work all day, but went everywhere with our company leader to flatter him. It gave everyone the same idea.

In 1975, when Deng Xiao Ping, the second highest Communist leader fell out of power, Shao came to our workshop section and said that Deng Xiao Ping will come back to power again. In 1977, this did in fact happen and Deng Xiao Ping was restored to his position as number-two man in China, but at this time Hua Guofeng had succeeded Mao upon his death. She also came to our workshop section and said that if "The Gang of Four" had come to power, our heads would have been cut off. I did not know her point in making these political statements, but working with her made me feel sick on a regular basis.

I do not know if readers in the US are familiar with a certain kind of political person. They are common in China and maybe all over the world. They often win promotions at high speed and they are a "winner" forever. During the Kuomintang times, they were Kuomintang members. When the Japanese occupied China, they were honored as helping Japan and being traitors to China. Now when Communism came into power, they some how became communist favorites. They always had to be on the winning side and they always gained a leadership position in an unusual way. This was especially troublesome during this time because the beliefs and goals of these three groups were not only different, but often in total opposition. To make such changes in values gave away their ultimate goal, to be in power.

In 1978, during the later half of the year with Deng Xiao Ping exerting his influence, the government began to reverse unjust verdicts of the past 30 years across the whole nation. Many of those purged during the Cultural Revolution were now considered "rehabilitated." This especially happened for those, such as I, who were called rightists. The actions started from the ministry of public security, which now had several former rightists who had served their sentence in Qinghai province. Early on there was a typical Chinese attempt at saving face so only certain people had their verdicts reversed. They deliberately kept many as rightists to somehow show the correctness of the anti-rightist struggle. Of course, decisions were made to remove or continue the rightist label based not as much on what the individual thought or said, but rather on how much the person was needed in various areas of the job market. Along with the trend of the times and the desire of the people they could not keep one rightist in the end.

Although the central government was determined to completely and rapidly improve this state of affairs, the party organizations at the local level did not willing do things in a frank and straightforward manor. The reason was that all these "unjust verdicts" were originally made by them and they were now being told to go against decisions they were earlier told to make. It seemed to the local Communist leaders that they were being asked to slap themselves in the face. Some of the leaders would not appear in public. Some of them argued that if all the previously "bad" people were emancipated how could control of the country continue and what would then happen? It was also argued that these newly-welcomed-back men could not be allowed to join the military or be asked to fight in a war because they could not be trusted to be loyal to Communism since obviously Communism had not been the least bit loyal to them. Second, these rightists can not be made to do manual work or to till the land. They could possibly do harm to people. Many had not been trained in a worthwhile way to achieve a livelihood so they could be used in the lowest of jobs.

Our company, at the end of 1978, had set up a rehabilitation team, but in the early stages they created all sorts of obstacles and difficulties. I tried wholeheartedly to understand thoroughly the true nature of the situation. The bottom line seemed to be that it was the trend of the times and how could you keep out the desire of hundreds of millions of Chinese people. My dossier finally in 1979, came up for consideration. I was made to report to the Xian court. The court comrade twice called me up and put questions to me. He took out my history which by now was about half a meter high. Within it were all my self criticisms, other information against me and confessions of my various companions. He also took out over fifty work reports and deeds my supervisors had summed up for me. (As you probably remember, in 1972, when the court pronounced me guilty, it was for only three causes). It gave me a start because some reports were grave, such as, when we had talked of running away to People's Republic of Mongolia. I did not remember all of the details that were reported. I admitted all the wrongs he mentioned, because I thought it would be best to go along and see what would happen.

Then this comrade of courts asked me other questions and he said that he needed to have my thoughts out in the open. He asked, "Do you on earth oppose the communist party?" I know he must put this question first. Obviously, in so many my materials, he only could find that I put a bad value on Mao, but I did speak highly of other party leaders. I answered, "Communism is a lofty ideal and it is highly idealistic." He then asked, "How is Communism wrong?" I replied that if I wanted to start a political party, it would surely be the Communist party just as the entire country had welcomed it in 1949. But, the heart of the matter is, who would lead such a party? Who is the real leader? Was it just Mao? And the "four men group"? Was the "five men group" leading also? What actually is the Communist Party? Is it the leaders or the people? Deng Xiao Ping was now the leader of the Communist party. (At that time I considered Ping to be a very good leader.) "Oh! I know what you are meaning!" he said, and added, "I tell you any expression of one's complex political views does not make one a counter revolutionary."

After several days, the Spring Festival or Chinese New Year was coming. This is our grandest festival of Chinese, also the longest vacation. Three days vacation plus the related Sunday and the actual Holiday made it five days long. These are the days that the Chinese family reunites. We look forward to this vacation for the entire year. Tomorrow will be year end and I have the day off. Today, after work, I first had to wash my work clothes in the workshop. By the time I had finished, it was 8 o'clock. I felt tired so I went to a back room to lie down and rest awhile before I would have dinner. Unexpectedly I found a note on the ground in the room. It was from the comrade of the court, asking me to go to court next day 8 a.m.

I arrived early. This comrade was not present, but was apparently going around the streets and notifying others to come today for their court verdict. He returned after half an hour. He must have typed all night because it looked like he had the results of several days work before him. He completed it all. He said, "I asked you to come today in order for you to have a happy spring festival." I listened carefully to him and I couldn't keep tears from pouring from my eyes and down my cheeks. There was at last a truly good person in the Communist party. I had met a few who were originally good persons but then their humanity would sink into oblivion when their superiors asked them to do bad things and they could do nothing but comply.

This was the best spring festival, the happiest day. Twenty-two years of my humiliating life had finally drawn to a complete end. I resumed my former title and wage. This was interesting and so surprising to find out my wages. They had not increased in these twenty-two years. Almost all intellectual's wages had not increased except a very few had been increased in 1963. As for workers' wages, in this twenty-two years they were only increased two or three times. My lost wages would not be reissued. But a big issue was made about my reflex camera amplifier and a little table which had been confiscated when guards searched my house. I was only allowed to have a bed, so they confiscated my property. My property was only the camera amplifier and a little table. But they said they had been sold for two yuan. I had bought these having spent my living expenses of one year (my living expenses of only twenty yuan a month). They wanted to return to me four yuan. What nerve! No sense of shame! I could not stop myself and said, "give it to my dear government as a present." I turned around and would leave, but they held me and said that they could not handle such comments. Did I want to be put in jail and start this over again?

At that time, other people were being newly taken as prisoners such as when the Red Guard searched houses and a soldier might secretly take a gold bar squeezed in his pocket. Another phenomenon in Shanghai at that time was that street cleaners often could find gold bars or jewelry in the trash (dust-bins). People were afraid that when their houses were searched and treasures were found they would go to prison. But, also if the street cleaner went off with the gold bar or jewelry and did not turn it in, for this he could suffer criticizism and be denounced. There were still many reasons to take people to prison.

In these twenty-two years, I had acted as electric worker, piping worker, scaffolder and building worker. With this change in my status, now my old friends and I would be able to get together at a public occasion. We were changed into humans from barely existing ghosts.

CHAPTER TWENTY-SEVEN:

MY SISTER'S PROBLEMS IN 1980

In the summer of 1980, I went home to the south to see my family. I discovered that for an unknown reason my second oldest sister after being reeducated through four years of labor did not have her verdict reversed yet. The heart of the matter was that there were no facts about a crime that she had committed. In essence, there was no verdict to reverse. This second sister had put forward her appeal to the higher authorities and they expressed that they did not know how to handle it. The reason was that she neither had committed a crime nor "wore a hat" which symbolized an "undesirable" person's status, as such landlord, bad element, rightist or counter revolutionary. How can we give her a statement of rehabilitation if she ad done nothing wrong to begin with?

The former organization where she had worked for thirty years had changed leaders many times and no one seemed to know why she was forced into rehabilitation. She had to run around to all administrative departments and the public health bureau, where they all showed concern. But, everyone was incapable of action. The government could not announce her rehabilitation, so she could not return to her former organization in which she had worked. She had no wages and was essentially jobless. After a year of trying, her organization had a new leader. After he read her dossier, he showed distress for her innocence and all the bad that had happened to her for no good reason. He made up his mind to help her settle this difficult problem. He made great efforts, got my sister's rehabilitation status and returned her to her former place of work. But, the irony of all this was that she returned in time to be retired. What an absolute waste of a talented woman!

Chapter Twenty-Eight:

My Lost Love

I had the opportunity to go to Shanghai where I had relatives, but also my former fiancée still lived there to my knowledge. I remember that the day was a Saturday and the weather was very hot. I rode on a trolley bus to my older brother's home. I was in a hurry because my younger brother was going to leave for Nanjing. I sat on a chair close to left window of the trolley bus, and wore sunglasses.

Unexpectedly, after I had returned to Xian, I received a letter from Shanghai. The graceful handwriting was familiar to me and made my heart race. It was from my former fiancée and she said that she had seen me in Shanghai on that Saturday on the trolley bus as it sped past her. She still recognized me after all these years. My heart beat even faster. This was not so simple, that after sixteen years had passed, in the twinkling of an eye, she could identify me wearing sunglasses. I was amazed. She went on to say that she thought that I was going to my oldest brother's home. She continued to go to her home because she didn't know how to get in touch with me. She couldn't remember my brother's house number. She intended to go the next day to my brother's street and try to find his home, but her daughter was ill and had to go to the hospital. Finally on Monday she found my brother's home and gave him this letter to send to me.

Can you guess what my feelings were? How would you feel? After sixteen years having a bosom filled with both love and grudges against her, I, in a moment, made a clean sweep of all bad feelings. I found a pen at once and wrote her a difficult letter explaining all the happenings of the past sixteen years. I sent the letter to her place of work. I held my breath for a month waiting for her reply. The more time that passed, the more I became filled with misgivings of another letter ever coming. Originally, when she wrote the former letter, she was on a business trip by herself to Beijing. Because she was still in Beijing, my letter was finally delivered to her mother by her work unit. Her mother, I know, had not learned to read. She did not know who the letter was from so she delivered my letter to her husband.

Then something unexpected happened, when she returned from her trip, her husband showed her the letter with a stern attitude waiting for her explanation. He had concluded that she was not being true to him. How could it be that she could not forget her former lover to still care enough to write and now he had written back to her. He was so upset that he even talked about the possibility of divorce. This was not what I wanted and certainly was not the intention of her letter or mine. Soon we communicated by telephone and agreed to meet at her youngest brother's home.

I had dreamed of this day so often during those sixteen years, but in a simple way. Things had gotten too complex and tense. My heart pounded so hard. She was coming. We looked at each other and smiled. It had been sixteen long years and I had been through a lot. She still looked the same. She was married and had two daughters. Her children were going to the junior school. I dare not treat her with hasty consideration. I did not want to become estranged from her again or put either of us in an awkward position. My feelings were so complex and totally indescribable. The seconds while I was waiting for her response seemed like hours. She greeted me with a smile, shook my hand and then embraced me. I embraced her tightly, like I had in the past. She told me of her life in the past sixteen years and it seemed to me like a movie.

In 1958, after we had broken off our friendship, there were still those two graduates coming from Nanjing, pursuing her at the same time. She was well disposed towards one and had a deep friendship and sense of trust. The other one was a secretary of the local Communist Youth League and often got into strong Marxism-Leninism discussions which made her both detest and fear him. Both men were putting pressure on her to make a decision and they came every Sunday to see if she had decided. When the Marxist entered the front door, the one she liked better left out the rear door because they both feared the Marxist and had a tacit understanding that they didn't know how she could end his interest without offending him and risking repercussions.

At last, she had no choice, but to be frank with him and she also told him about me and that she still felt close to me. He showed comprehension of her difficulties, but obviously felt he had less of a chance to win her heart. After awhile this man married another woman, but they continued their friendship even after his marriage. In 1964, when she finally thought she had gotten over the love relationship with me, he expressed his feelings of regret that if he'd known this before hand he really wanted to marry her. He was not happy, but felt he could not end his marriage.

In 1965, she had another boyfriend. I told her that I knew about this man because he was my brother's schoolmate and had told my brother of his interest in her. Her parents really liked this man and were hoping she would finally be getting married.

When the Cultural Revolution began, her family felt very anxious that there might be a search their house and their property would be confiscated again. Back in 1953, her father was considered a "law breaking capitalist" and had been criticized and denounced. All his property had been confiscated and they were removed from their house. In all the many years since that her father had not gone back to work. But, the Communist party never seems to forget old accounts and they were scared to death. For some reason her parents gave several gold bars and the jewelry that they kept hidden in 1953 to the boyfriend. He was to pass these things on to his aunt who was considered working class and would never be suspected of having anything valuable. She had agreed to keep the valuables safe and hidden until the danger appeared to be passed. Who would have thought, they were courting disaster and his aunt, as it turned out was steadfast in her proletarian stand and turned everything over to the higher authorities. Immediately their house was searched and all their property, even that of little value was confiscated. Their entire family including siblings owned three houses which were all confiscated too. They were left with one small house for everyone to share. The entire family would have been left homeless except that her father was a cripple and couldn't take care of himself. This was a rare example of the Communist Party having sympathy on someone. Obviously the relationship between her and my brother's schoolmate came to a dramatic end. This time her parents remembered me. They said they knew I would have never done such things.

At this time in Shanghai, street cleaners could find gold bars, jewelry and other treasures in trash containers along the street. Owners of such valuables were afraid of having their houses searched because if such things were found, you could not be sure of the result.

Finally in 1968, she married a man ten years older than she who was a teacher of a special classification. I told her that I knew this because my eldest sister had told me. It happened that my youngest sister from Beijing had come to Shanghai and saw them together in a restaurant. They all thought that you married him because he was a teacher of a special classification that was called a reactionary learning authority. Her father had to move to the countryside to be remolded and before leaving, her father and her husband wept face to face when he promised to take care of both his wife and her mother. Her father could set his mind at rest and go alone, knowing that his wife would be taken care of and had a new family.

In 1969, the man she formerly was seeing who was the Secretary of the Communist Youth League decided that he now hated her because she had married another. In her work place he forced her to put up Da Zi Bao, propagated her place as a league member and was at one time in love with a rightist. She was kept apart from co-workers and investigated.

She also told me about when she was eight months pregnant and her father died. She was allowed to take his dead body. That day there was heavy rain like you might see in a TV drama. She told of having such a big belly and having difficulty just getting about. She struggled to handle the body which had been placed on a cart. When she arrived at her parent's old home there was only one room left for the family. When all the sons and daughters arrived, eleven people filled the room with the father's dead body on a cart parked in the center. So many members of the family came, but there was no place they could sleep. At night there was no alternative but for some family members to sleep in a courtyard under a big plastic sheet while others slept inside beside the dead body. It rained the entire time with strong wailing winds and weeping rain, sharing and adding to the grief.

Within a week we met three times at her two younger brothers' homes and once in the park where we could talk alone. We decided that we had been separated from each other too long of a time with too much happening in each of our lives for us to be able to continue a romantic love. We seemed to have gone beyond that, but we would always care deeply about the other and remain friends. She really needed to stay with her husband and daughters. I needed to go on with my life. I had decided while in prison that I was not going to allow the early wasted years of my life make the later years also a disaster. I wanted to still find love, marry and have a child. I wanted as full a life as possible after my early years had been so totally wasted.

Chapter Twenty-Nine:

True Love and a Full Life

In 1981, came our Spring Festival or Chinese New Year. Our company workshop needed an improved electric furnace transformer. I was in charge of this engineering project. During the holidays there was an opportunity to step up the work that had to be done while the furnace didn't need to be used. The company sent a young woman who specialized as an electric welder to work with me. For two days we worked at full tilt and basically forget the holiday. During the second day of spring festival we were working hard again and I got an idea that if we didn't take lunch at the regular time we could break early from the day and have a nice late lunch without having to return to work. She agreed to the proposal that we work until 3 p.m. that day. We got so much work done and we seemed to function very well together. Because of the holiday I could find no place for her to buy lunch because the company's restaurant as well as all the other nearby restaurants which mostly served workers, stopped serving for the holiday. I told her that I had an egg shaped briquette stove at my dormitory and I invited her to come and cook rice with me. Thus we began to get to know each other personally. We already knew how pleasantly and well we worked together. There were three days left of the holiday and neither of us had time enough to be with our families or do anything else to celebrate the New Year. We really enjoyed cooking together and one afternoon we went to the park. The next day we spent the entire day together, cooking and walking around. As you can probably tell, we were falling in love.

My soon-to-be wife was quite a bit younger than I, which was great with me because I still hoped to have a child. Her parents, in the 1950s had lived in Shanghai and then were relocated to China's great northwest at Xian where she was brought up. In 1974, she graduated from middle school then went to the countryside to work. In November of 1977, she moved to our company and worked in the same large shop as I did, but at that time we had not noticed each other.

Three months later, I asked her parents for their consent that we be married. The day of our wedding was a sunlit and enchanting spring day. We came out of the marriage registry office and went directly to the park to celebrate our becoming a couple, husband and wife. There were ripples on the lake and birds sang on the willow branches. All of nature seemed to give us a blessing. And we in fact have had over twenty years of happiness and joy.

I so cherished the memory of my earlier life in the south that I asked the Communist Party to be transferred to my hometown. My thought was that for the past thirty years where the party pointed I rushed at their command, sometimes obviously not having a choice, but now I first put forward this demand. I wanted to go to Hangzhou or to Shanghai, but it was impossible. But then I was offered a position in another city which is west of Shanghai and was close enough to Hangzhou, to take advantage of frequent reunions with my brothers and sisters.

Later that year, we were moved to that city. The personnel division there said that my file was about a meter thick. It seems my "black materials" were never removed or burned which had been stipulated. The organization in which one works must hold a meeting to announce a person's rehabilitation and then burn up his black materials. In the summer of 1979, my company surely held a rehabilitation meeting, where it was announced that after twenty years I had finally completed rehabilitation. But, nothing else had been done.

But, this seemed good enough that I was being given a fresh start. I, at last, had a job where I could use my excellent education. I was teaching engineering at a small university. It was such a rewarding and fulfilling position. I loved working with the young students.

CHAPTER THIRTY:

LOOKING BACK

So, now you know my life from its beginning in south China to my first work experience in the northeast, then to the northwest for reeducation passing through different prisons and a work farm for twenty years and now back to central China to finally have a meaningful work and life.

The worst thing that I experienced by far and was almost unable to endure was not eating, severe hunger and at times, starvation. My eating habits changed so radically over time. When I first went to the northeast the food seemed so different from what I had eaten in Central China. The steamed breads smelled sour and the new dishes were hard to swallow. Eating lunch at the company was so unusual because there were no tables or stools to sit on. We had to become used to having lunch squatting down. I, as a human did not think we should eat like that. I certainly do not think that humans should live like I was forced to live for too many years. By 1954, things were worse when too often I was close to death when rice or even camel grass nearly could not be found.

Now I am advanced in years and feeling as if I soon will be a falling leaf which settles near the roots. Political problems in China have thoroughly settled. I was finally able to use my education and intellectual capacity to teach at a university for ten years before I arrived at retirement age. But they were ten wonderful and fulfilling years training engineers many of whom eventually worked on the great

Three Gorges Dam. I actually only worked fifteen years of my life at what I consider actual jobs, where I was hired and paid a wage. All the rest of my years in forced labor were, of course, more difficult and lamentable.

Now I live a stable life and my wife and I had a lovely daughter who is already eighteen years old and nearly graduated from a senior middle school. My sole aspiration in life is that she will be admitted to an ideal college after doing well on her examination.

I'll always remember the days of the prime years of my life, especially the years in prison. I will never get over the anger that I feel for how so much of my life was wasted. I don't know why the Communist Government had to so cruelly mistreat common people. We were the very own sons and daughters of China. We meant no harm except to express our thoughts and ideas. Why they treated us as they did, I will never comprehend. There were so many horrifying atrocities far worse than what happened to me and what I've shared with you. Their actions were beyond the comprehension of both Chinese, also foreigners, who will someday know all that happened. Like a nightmarish demon this weighs down my heart and can not find relief.

I have often watched with great interest on TV about foreign jails and prisons. Usually prisoners had beds with enough space to move about. Especially wonderful, there are flush toilets. People were not made to defecate on the ground like domesticated animals. Prison guards treat prisoners with due respect. It made my heart beat faster with wonder and amazement. In America, prisoners did not have to work long hours and have enough free time to act on their own, even having a library with books to read and study. That made me so envious, if only I had had books to read. I would have read every book I could get my hands on.

In the 1990s I had read a news article in China that satirized the French prison system blowing their own trumpet that their prisons are the most reliable in the world. They have the most advanced facilities to ensure that prisoners cannot run away and do not even want to. But there was a prisoner who still tried to run away from this jail. This prisoner used a red cloth as an identification signal to a helicopter hired for his escape. I also watched the TV version of this news and it showed prisoners, to my surprise, playing football and that is where he got the red flag. How could we Chinese who had been in our prisons imagine such a sight? The thought of this kind of prison and this situation made me distressed at all the horrible treatment I had received. The part that grieves me the most is that I never really was a criminal as other men who are jailed in the rest of the world. My crime was to think freely, to feel injustice and to expect more from my government.

Many of my family members and my closest friends often tried patiently to talk with me in the hope that their caring would help me overcome the psychic trauma I had experienced. They believed that mostly time could pacify my psychic trauma. But twenty years have passed and time has not helped me when I see the unfairness in the world. Government officials, not only in China, but in other countries in the world are allowed to run on a rampage hurting whoever they want. I cannot restrain my indignant heart whenever I hear of man's inhumanity to others. I am not simply grieved by my own past record, but also whenever I hear of others who have died or maybe live in tragic conditions beyond compare in this human world. Often it makes what happened to me as nothing compared to other stories. Many others, too, have experienced pain because of our nationalities. I know that what happened to me was because I lived in China at a terrible time in our history. People all over the world have made a submission to oppression. They must decide if they would rather kneel in order to live rather than stand up and have to die.

When will we humans wake up to reality?

There will be an end to such injustices when humans learn from our past mistakes that we, in fact, all are one.

<<All this my lifetime>>

THE END!

Epilogue

After I left China, Robert and I occasionally kept in touch by e-mail. We tried to communicate in what we thought were secret words and vague expressions that we both hopefully understood. I would mostly tell him of the writing progress that I was making. He mostly told about his poor health. Each winter after I left China he would become ill with severe lung problems and pneumonia. He often wrote that he had been in the hospital.

In 2004, a friend of mine published a book with iUniverse and I knew that there would definitely be a way for me to publish the information that Robert had given me. My last message to him included words that said "our success was assured" and "I've found the way to fulfill the promise that I made to you." My last message was very positive, hopeful and happy that the dream Robert had had for almost the past fifty years would be accomplished.

I have come to the conclusion that Robert died the winter of 2004. I do not know if he first received my message. I never received a reply from him. I still have hope that I may someday hear from his daughter or perhaps the friend whose computer he used to write to me.

I believe that he knew this book would be published and that allowed him to pass on with fulfillment and peace in his heart.

In Appreciation

Since I am using a pseudonym I cannot name the people who I want to thank for helping and supporting me in writing this book. You know who you are and I think you know of my sincere appreciation and gratefulness for many suggestions, words of encouragement and help. I want to thank my partner who has taught me much about injustice and especially my children and grandchildren who have insured my investment in the future of humanity.

None of us will be named here, just as the names of millions of dead Chinese people in the Laogai will remain unknown. In our hearts we know what we have done to help the cause of justice in the world. I believe that it is the best that we can do, to leave the world a better place as a result of our brief time here.

I also want to refer interested readers to the books written by Harry Wu as shown in my bibliography. His Laogai Research Foundation is worth learning about. The web-site is: http//www.laogai.org.

Harry Wu and his team are doing so much to make the world aware of China's past so we all can be wiser in the future. I am thankful for all the work that Mr. Wu has done and I hope that I have contributed my part to this cause.

junemudan@yahoo.com

Bibliography

Binyab, Liu, *Tell the World—What Happened In China and Why*, New York, Random House, 1989.

Blunden, Caroline and Elvin, Mark, *Cultural Atlas of China*, New York, Facts On File, 1983.

Chesneaux, Jean, *China The People's Republic 1949–1976*, New York, Random House, 1979.

DeCrespigny, Rafe, *China This Century*, New York, Oxford University Press, 1992.

Dudley, William and Karin Swisher, *China-Opposing Viewpoints*, San Diego, CA, Greenhaven Press, Inc. 1989.

Fishman, Ted, *China, Inc.*, New York, Schribner, 2005.

Human Rights in China, *Children of the Dragon*, New York, MacMillan Publishing Company, 1989.

Lieberthal, Kenneth, *Governing China*, New York, London, WW Norton & Company, Inc. 1995.

Ogden, Suzanne, *China's Unresolved Issues*, Englewood Cliffs, New Jersey, Prentice Hall, 1995.

Salisbury, Harrison, *The New Emperors—China in the Era of Mao and Deng*, Boston, Little, Brown and Company, 1992.

Solzhenitsyn, Alexander, *Gulag Archipelago*, New York, Harper and Row, 1985.

Storey, Robert; Goncharoff, Nicko; Harper, Damian; Cambon, Marie; Huhti, Thomas; Liou, Caroline; English, Alexander, *China*, Australia, Lonely Planet Publications,1998.

Terrill, Ross, *The China Difference,* New York, Harper & Row, Publishers, 1979.

Thurston, Anne, *A Chinese Odyssey-The Life and Times of a Chinese Dissident*, New York, Charles Schribner's Sons, 1991.

Wintle, Justin, *The Timeline History of China*, New York, Barnes and Noble, 2002.

Wu, Harry, *Troublemaker*, New York, Times Books, A Division of Random House, Inc., 1998.

Wu, Harry, *Bitterwinds*, New York, John Wiley and Sons, Inc.,1994.

Wu, Hongda Harry, *Laogai The Chinese Gulag*, Boulder, Westview Press,1992.

About the Author

June Mudan is the pseudonym for an American teacher who received Masters Degrees from the University of Wisconsin and the University of Colorado. She has taught in several states over her twenty-five year career in the United States.

978-0-595-45516-4
0-595-45516-6